CALIFORNIA NATURAL HISTORY GUIDES

INTRODUCTION TO FIRE
IN CALIFORNIA

California Natural History Guides

Phyllis M. Faber and Bruce M. Pavlik, General Editors

Introduction to

FIRE

in California

David Carle

UNIVERSITY OF CALIFORNIA PRESS

Berkeley   Los Angeles   London

This one is for Greg, a fire captain, for Ed, a fire chief, and in memory of Harold Biswell, a pioneer in prescribed fire.

University of California Press, one of the most distinguished university presses in the United States, enriches lives around the world by advancing scholarship in the humanities, social sciences, and natural sciences. Its activities are supported by the UC Press Foundation and by philanthropic contributions from individuals and institutions. For more information, visit www.ucpress.edu.

California Natural History Guide Series, No. 95

University of California Press
Berkeley and Los Angeles, California

University of California Press, Ltd.
London, England

© 2008 by the Regents of the University of California

Library of Congress Cataloging-in-Publication Data

Carle, David, 1950–
  Introduction to fire in California / David Carle.
    p. cm. — (California natural history guides ; no. 95)
  Includes bibliographical references and index.
  ISBN 978-0-520-24873-1 (cloth : alk. paper) — ISBN 978-0-520-25577-7 (pbk. : alk. paper)
    1. Wildfires — California. 2. Forest fires — California. 3. Fire ecology — California. I. Title.

SD421.32.C2C38 2008
634.9′61809794 — dc22   2007037339

Manufactured in China
16 15 14 13 12 11 10 09 08
10 9 8 7 6 5 4 3 2 1

The paper used in this publication meets the minimum requirements of ANSI/NISO Z39.48–1992 (R 1997)(*Permanence of Paper*).

Although the University of California Press and the author have made every attempt to ensure that the information in this book is accurate, they are not responsible for any loss, damage, injury, or inconvenience that may occur to anyone as a result of using this book. Following the advice in this book does not guarantee protection against fire risk. You are responsible for your own safety, as well as the safety of your home, property, and belongings.

Cover photograph: A prescribed burn clears the understory and small-diameter trees in a Jeffrey-pine forest. Photo by Pete Hein.

The publisher gratefully acknowledges the generous
contributions to this book provided by

the Gordon and Betty Moore Fund
in Environmental Studies
and
the General Endowment Fund of the
University of California Press Foundation.

CONTENTS

ACKNOWLEDGMENTS

Two books that were published by the University of California Press in 2006 were particularly timely and helpful resources as I prepared this book: *Fire in California Ecosystems* is a comprehensive textbook, coedited by Neil G. Sugihara, Jan W. van Wagtendonk, JoAnn Fites-Kaufman, Kevin E. Shaffer, and Andrea E. Thode; and *Introduction to Chaparral in California*, by Ronald D. Quinn and Sterling C. Keeley, is in the California Natural History Guide series and devotes attention to the role of fire in chaparral and the challenges for humans living in that environment.

My sincere thanks for close reading of the manuscript and helpful suggestions go to Dr. Jan van Wagtendonk, research forester at the U.S. Geological Survey Yosemite Field Station; Dr. Connie Millar, U.S. Forest Service scientist at the Pacific Southwest Field Station in Albany; Dr. James K. Agee, in the College of Forest Resources at the University of Washington; Dr. Neil G. Sugihara, U.S. Forest Service regional fire ecologist; Tom Higley, retired U.S. Forest Service silviculturist; Sally Gaines; Dr. Rick Kattelmann (who also provided six photographs for this book); and, always, Janet Carle, my wife and first reader.

Editors Jenny Wapner and Kate Hoffman have made it a real pleasure to produce this third of my books for the University of California Press, in the California Natural History Guide series. Thanks, also, to copy editor Meg Hannah.

INTRODUCTION

Pile some kindling and small logs in a fireplace so that the bit of paper underneath will send its heat upward after it is lit. Strike a match. Quickly tilt it so that the flame burns up along this tiny bit of fuel between your fingers, so the match flares strongly enough to pass fire to the wood. Or to the charcoal in a backyard barbecue. Or to the pine needles and twigs within a circle of rocks forming a campfire ring. Or, perhaps, simply to a candlewick, which flares, flickers, and then persists. Light emerges from wick and wax, energy suddenly made visible. Heat also appears that had been trapped within that fuel, hidden until that moment.

Light and heat are basic attributes of the familiar process of fire. Flames can be comforting and useful when tamed to our will. But this is a wild force, too, one that can roam across the landscape, transforming matter, returning often enough to shape adaptations by plants and animals, and sometimes delivering unstoppable destruction to human communities.

Need it even be said that fire is neither bad nor good, in itself? It is one of the natural, inevitable processes of this earth. We, too, are creatures shaped by fire, using it more purposefully than any other species.

Fire, as our tool, melts, reshapes, cuts, heats, cooks, emits light, and propels us over the ground or through the air. Obvious fires burn in furnaces and smelters, welder's arcs and acetylene torches. More subtle uses trap fire out of sight in our internal combustion engines, or where small pilot lights hide beneath gas water heaters and stoves, waiting to awaken heating elements and burners.

So many examples in our lives reveal our special relationship with fire. Homes, factories, and business buildings may be equipped with fire extinguishers, smoke alarms, and overhead sprinklers. Career firefighters staff fire stations with specialized fire engines and fire gear. Where communities are too small for that extravagance, volunteer fire departments are organized to fill the need. By the start of each year's fire season, seasonal wildland firefighters are hired and trained as hotshots and smokejumpers, hand crews, hose crews, and tower lookouts. Dozer operators and highly trained aircraft pilots are put on call.

Though preparation for fires permeates our lives, when they finally arrive it is usually a shock, as if our secret thought all along was *fire will never happen to me.* A woman who lost her home in the wildfire that raced through the Oakland Hills in 1991 exclaimed, "We had sidewalks! The way people talk about the fire area, you would think I was Little Red Riding Hood living in the forest!" (Sullivan 1993, 23). Her amazement, after learning that modern urban life could be so disrupted by wildfire (pl. 1), illustrates one value of a book about fire in California.

Over eight million Californians live at similar risk, near the edge of wildlands subject to periodic wildfires (map 1). They need to understand this aspect of their environment. Ignorance about fire, as the population has grown and sprawled, has contributed to increased structural damage losses and lost lives from wildfires. This book is meant to help humanity understand its place in the California landscape as another one of many fire-adapted species in this state.

"The Nature of Fire" opens with the question, "What is fire?" A detailed answer includes the aspects of the fire triangle: fuel, oxygen, and heat. Almost all fires are ignited either by lightning or by human activities. The many ways that California Indians used fire are explained, as are ways that weather and topography influence fire behavior.

Fire ecology is the focus of the next section, "Fire and Life across California," detailing adaptations to fire regimes affecting California's variety of vegetation types and wildlife, and its soil, water, and air resources. Impacts of climate change on

Plate 1. One of the Oakland Hills houses burned in the Tunnel fire of 1991.

relationships between fire and natural landscapes are an emerging part of the story.

During the last century, California events played central roles in shaping national fire policies and attitudes about wildfire. "Flames of History" tells about the state's "light-burning" debate early in the twentieth century. Threats to West Coast forests during World War II helped bring Smokey Bear into being. And an overview of major wildfires in California history includes those that burned the most acres and houses, or were most deadly to people.

The missions and responsibilities, tactics and weaponry of firefighting organizations and land management agencies are the opening topics of "Burning Issues," followed by policy changes aimed at "Making Peace" by restoring fire to the landscape with prescribed burns, where feasible. Many Californians live in chaparral, where the fire regime delivers intense crown fires. A debate among scientists about the relative importance of fuel accumulation versus extreme fire weather,

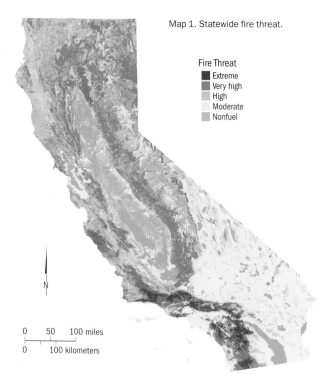

Map 1. Statewide fire threat.

Fire Threat
- ■ Extreme
- ■ Very high
- High
- Moderate
- Nonfuel

N

0   50   100 miles
0   100 kilometers

especially wind, in driving chaparral wildfires is explained, along with the ramifications for fire management. State and national fire plans aim at solutions to the challenges of wildfire and paint a statistical picture of where we are in those efforts. Timber harvest versus a mix of thinning and burning to reduce fire risk is a current contentious issue.

"Getting Ready" shifts to personal responsibilities of Californians living on the edge of wildlands. "Fire-Safe Planning" in the wildland-urban interface zone includes suggestions about what to do before, during, and after fires.

My interest in these topics took root, as it has for many Californians, because of a personal experience with the drama and tragedy of Southern California wildfires. In my senior year in high school, our family home was one of dozens that burned during a large, Santa Ana wind–driven wildfire that swept across the hills of Orange County. It is probably just co-incidence that a brother became a fire captain with the city of Los Angeles, a brother-in-law was the fire chief of El Cajon, and more recently, one of my sons staffed a Forest Service fire lookout tower during the summer fire season. Though part of a small community's volunteer fire department, I have never been employed as a firefighter. Basic training in fire ecology and experience with prescribed burns came along with a career as a California State Park Ranger. For several years, I led guided walks for the public and for school children through recently burned areas in the Sierra Nevada foothills, where oak trees, grasses, and shrubs revealed their survival tactics. In 2002, my environmental history book, *Burning Questions*, was published, covering the last century's debates over national wildland policy and prescribed burning.

Introduction to Fire in California is the third book in a sub-series of the California Natural History Guides that focuses on Californians and Their Environment, following books on water and air. They are natural history books that recognize the overwhelming role of humanity in California's environment. As short introductions, they must be concise summaries of complex subjects. A number of professional fire-fighters, fire ecologists, foresters, and other scientists (named in the acknowledgments) scrutinized the manuscript so that simplification might not lead to inaccuracies.

In a 1980 speech by a pioneering fire ecologist at the University of California School of Forestry, Dr. Harold Biswell made suggestions that may help us appreciate our place on a long list of fire-adapted species in California: "Keep in mind that fire is a natural part of the environment, about as important as rain and sunshine. Fire has always been here and everything good evolved with it…[so] we must work more in harmony with nature, not so much against it" (Biswell 1980, 1).

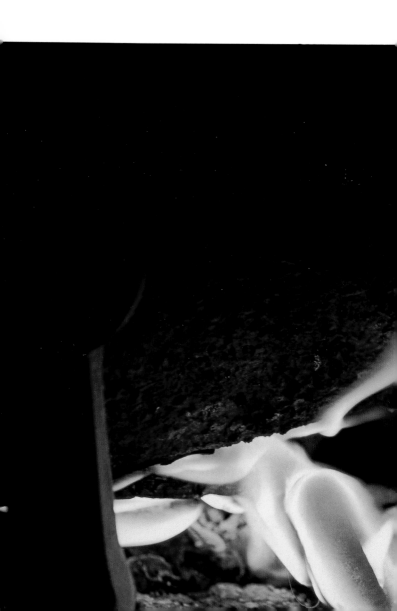

For flame is par excellence Fire: but flame is burning smoke, and smoke consists of Air and Earth.

—ARISTOTLE, 350 B.C., BOOK 2, PART 4

Things fall apart; the centre cannot hold.

—WILLIAM BUTLER YEATS, 1921

What Is Fire?

Though a familiar presence throughout our lives, the essence of burning still seems mysterious. What is happening as flames quietly crackle or, sometimes, roar with the powerful voice of energy unleashed? What is this thing called "fire"?

To Aristotle and other ancient Greeks, fire was an agent that imposed forms on the remaining fundamental elements: earth, air, and water. Though we no longer think of fire as an "element," the idea that it is a transforming agent is very familiar to modern fire ecologists. Fire on the California landscape has shaped evolutionary adaptations of both plants and animals.

Combustion, another name for fire, is an energy-releasing chemical reaction that, once initiated, can become self-perpetuating. When enough heat is generated to make the fire "contagious," nearby fuels are dried and their temperature increases. At the ignition temperature, chemical bonds between carbon and hydrogen break. It is vaporized molecules, rather than the solid fuel, that actually ignite in flaming combustion as the gaseous fuel cloud reacts with oxygen in the air. That oxidation (yet another name for burning) produces carbon dioxide and water.

Much slower oxidation burns within the cells of plants and animals, whose aerobic metabolisms break down food for cellular energy. Rusting metal is yet another example of oxidation occurring too slowly to give off noticeable heat.

The heat generated as wildlands burn reveals how much sunlight energy was captured and stored by plants during photosynthesis. Though the maximum potential yield is never achieved (because wildfires do not produce complete combustion), and significant energy always goes toward evaporation of water, phenomenal heat releases still occur. Flames that tower 100 feet into the sky visually suggest that scale (pl. 2). In wildfires with just 12-foot flame lengths, every yard along

Plate 2. A wall of flame burns through desert shrubs and Joshua trees as a California Department of Forestry and Fire Protection (CAL FIRE) truck monitors the Sawtooth Complex wildfire of 2006.

the leading edge of the fire may generate 4,000 kilowatts of heat energy, the equivalent of 4,000 single-bar electric heaters stacked on top of each other. A domestic example is revealing: the energy in one cord of dry firewood can equal that in 160 gallons of gasoline (a stacked cord is four feet wide, eight feet long, and four feet high).

Fire is one way that vegetation energy and molecular complexity succumb to the second law of thermodynamics. According to that law of physics, energy tends to disperse from where it is concentrated, and randomness, ultimately, increases. Since fire breaks complex molecules down to simpler forms, it is a type of decomposition, releasing and recycling nutrients. In fact, in dry climates like those found across much of California, fire has been the primary agent of decomposition.

Flames are the visible evidence of fire (pl. 3). Their glowing light comes from particles of soot—unburned carbon—heated to incandescence. The particular colors that are radiated depend on temperature. In most wildland fires, yellow and orange predominate, with more red appearing as the fire cools. White and blue flames are hottest but more often are seen outside wildland settings in fires stoked with bellows or when flammable liquids burn. A pattern of colors corresponding to energy levels is similarly apparent in rainbows, which reveal the spectrum of energy levels in white light: lowest-energy bands are red, and energy increases through progressive color bands toward the blue and violet ranges.

Plate 3. Flame is the visible evidence of fire.

Smoke commonly appears with flames because combustion is never complete. Soot rising away from the hottest parts of the fire in heated air is visible as black smoke. Smoke (pl. 4) that is whiter includes steaming water evaporated from the fuel.

Plate 4. Different colors of smoke reflect different moisture levels and types of burning fuels.

Plate 5. Ash builds up as a fire smolders, because combustion is never completely efficient.

The gaseous flaming phase eventually collapses back onto solid fuel, and then heat can continue gnawing away at a log as glowing combustion. Ash residues (pl. 5) of noncombustible materials, such as silica, are another sign that the burning process is never completely efficient. Ashes can pile up and smother fires, putting them out if they block access to oxygen. So, we stir campfires as they burn down and must regularly clean ashes from fireplaces and woodstoves.

The Fire Triangle

The basic requirements for fire are often summarized as a triangle whose three sides are oxygen, fuel, and heat (fig. 1). Firefighters are taught to put out fires by eliminating any one of the triangle's sides. They can shovel dirt onto flames to smother them, depriving them of oxygen, for example. Often they will scrape a line down to bare soil around a fire to deprive it of new fuel. Or, they might use water to cool a fire down below its ignition temperature.

Oxygen: Fire Breath

Though the predominant gas in Earth's atmosphere is nitrogen, the 21 percent that is oxygen gas is key in processes that cycle energy. The oxygen molecule is very reactive. Not content to stay in that O_2 form, it is always ready to react chemically with other molecules it encounters. That reaction is called oxidation.

Scientist James Lovelock has speculated that oxygen concentrations above 25 percent would make *everything* flammable, even damp wood; but if the level fell below 15 percent, not even the driest twigs would burn. If oxygen levels were

Figure 1. The fire triangle: fires require heat to work on fuel in the presence of oxygen.

too low, there would not be enough to support metabolic respiration, but if too high, the reactive nature of oxygen would destroy living cells.

The atmospheric concentration of oxygen is maintained partly by life forms in an elegant balance between respiration and photosynthesis. Through photosynthesis (literally, "making with light"), green plants use solar energy to transform carbon dioxide and water into glucose. That product is then used by plants to ultimately build the complex carbon molecules of stems, leaves, flowers, and roots. So, photosynthesis transforms light energy into reservoirs of chemical energy. Oxygen gas is a waste product for plants, released to the atmosphere during photosynthesis.

Respiration, by both animals and plants, reverses the photosynthesis equation. Oxygen reacts with complex carbon molecules, releasing carbon dioxide, water, and energy. You are reading these words and turning the pages of this book by utilizing chemical energy from metabolic respiration. Breathe in oxygen, exhale carbon dioxide, and participate in the elegant balance.

Fire also reverses the photosynthesis equation, but more rapidly than metabolic respiration, with energy from fires released as heat and light.

Fuel: Fire Food

Fuels are anything that can burn. Much of fire ecology and firefighting focuses on the character of fuels and on fuel treatments (pl. 6). Moisture levels are one key to fuel flammability. The size of fuel pieces and their vertical arrangement are other important factors.

Wet or damp wood is, of course, not the fuel desired when building a campfire. Before it will burn, all the fuel's moisture has to be evaporated away. Nor can a fire be started by applying a tiny match to great big logs. Success comes from work-

Plate 6. Scraping a fire line.

ing with small kindling, whose increased surface area dries out faster and makes it easier to heat to its ignition temperature. Once ignited, larger pieces can be added, generating more heat as the fire grows, until it eventually becomes self-sustaining.

In the same way, fine, light fuels on wildlands lose moisture more quickly to the air than do thick, woody fuels. Increased surface area also exposes more area to oxygen, letting those fine fuels ignite readily and burn more intensely. In California, chamise *(Adenostoma fasciculatum)*(pl. 7), a widespread chaparral shrub, is commonly used to calculate fuel moisture levels. Fuel moisture is a measure of water content relative to the dry weight of the fuel. Samples are weighed, then dried and weighed again. A 100 percent measurement means the water in the stems equaled the dry weight of the fuel (or 50 percent of the sample's initial weight). If two-thirds of the weight of the fuel is water, the fuel has a 200 percent moisture level. In California's pattern of wet winters and

Plate 7. Chamise, the most widespread chaparral shrub in California.

dry summers, live fuel moisture readings of 160 percent in June can drop to 40 percent by September. Dead fuel readings might be less than three percent.

Fuel moisture monitoring is important when calculating daily fluctuations of fire season danger levels and is a key when conducting prescribed burns. Fire professionals also classify and monitor so-called time-lag fuels, based on the way

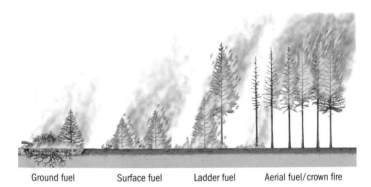

| Ground fuel | Surface fuel | Ladder fuel | Aerial fuel/crown fire |

Figure 2. Fuel types: ground, surface, ladder, and crown.

different fuel diameters respond to moisture changes in the atmosphere. In this system, one-hour time-lag fuels are small branches, forest litter, or detritus from zero to one fourth of an inch in diameter that react to hourly changes in humidity; 10-hour fuels are a fourth to one inch in diameter and respond to day-to-day changes in moisture levels; 100-hour fuels have one- to three-inch diameters and take several days to change; and 1,000-hour fuels are three to eight inches or more in diameter and can take a whole season to respond to humidity changes.

Vertical arrangements are another way to characterize different wildfire fuel categories (fig. 2). Ground fuels burn with slowly moving fires that smolder in the duff and litter. Surface fuels feed fires that travel through "dead and down" woody materials, grasses, and shrubs on the surface (pl. 8). Ladder fuels are tall shrubs or small trees beneath the taller forest canopy that will carry fire up into the canopy and lead to crown fires. Crown fuels burn within the canopy overstory of

Plate 8. Ground litter builds up and becomes fuel for fire.

forests or shrub fields; a crown fire can burn into the top of a single plant or move actively along through the forest or shrub canopy.

While this section has focused on wildland fire fuels, homes and other human structures are also potential fire fuel. We transform trees into lumber, a dry, dead, and flammable form of vegetation. Ways to reduce that flammability and risk are covered in "Getting Ready: Life on the Edge."

Heat: Fire Energy

Heat can be transferred via conduction, radiation, or convection. Conduction passes heat energy along from molecule to molecule, as when the heat of a fire moves along a branch or a

Plate 9. Heat is transferred from a wood-stove fire to a teapot and fire poker by conduction, up the stovepipe and out the spout of the pot by convection, and into the room by radiation.

fireplace poker, or a hot woodstove surface passes heat into a tea kettle. Radiation energy travels as a ray or energy wave across space to heat wildland fuels ahead of a flaming front or to warm someone close to that woodstove. Convection is the movement of heated molecules, usually upward, to where they transfer their energy. Convection sends heat from the stove up toward the ceiling and causes smoke to rise through the stovepipe, and steam to waft from the spout of a boiling tea kettle (pl. 9).

Fires will go out if the heat element of the fire triangle is broken by cooling fuel down to below its ignition temperature. Water works particularly well for this, since water molecules absorb so much heat before changing from liquid to vapor. At 212°F, the boiling point of water, steam forms and carries away the heat it has absorbed. Steam can also smother fires by displacing oxygen in the air close to the fuel.

Ignition Sources

Whether started with a match, by lightning, or by a volcanic eruption, an ignition source must first dry out any moisture in the fuels and then heat the fuels to their ignition points. Chemists describe that initial energy requirement as the activation energy needed to get the chemical reaction of burning under way.

Lightning is a natural ignition source that is unevenly distributed across this state (map 2). From 1985 through 2000, over one million lightning strikes were detected in California (pl. 10). Nearly half of those struck in the southeastern deserts. Lightning strikes peak in the interior mountain ranges in August. During six years, 7,250 strikes were detected inside Yosemite National Park, ranging from 530 to 2,016 per year, and focused primarily from June through September (van Wagtendonk and Cayan 2007). California's central coast, however, has the lowest incidence of lightning strikes anywhere in the country.

Most strikes do not start a fire. The Coast Ranges experience more of their lightning during the winter and spring, when fuels are wetter, so those lightning strikes are less likely to start a fire. Only five percent of the detected Yosemite strikes ignite fires. Dry lightning storms are more likely to ignite fires than summer monsoonal thunderstorms, which coincide with rain in the deserts and the Sierra Nevada.

Humans are the other major wildfire ignition source in California. Humanity evolved using fire as a tool. For over 9,000 years, California Indians set fires to manage the land-

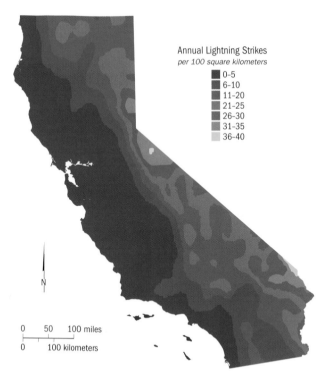

Map 2. Lightning-strike frequency patterns across California.

Plate 10. A lightning ground-strike just misses a tree.

scape. "Fire was the most significant, effective, efficient, and widely employed vegetation management tool of California Indian tribes" (Anderson 2005, 136). They burned to reduce the threat of wildfires near their villages, to stimulate resprouting of straighter stems needed for basketry (pl. 11), to keep meadows and grasslands from converting to shrublands or forests while stimulating the growth of seeds and bulbs used as food (pl. 12), to control insects and fungus in important foods such as acorns, to increase forage (both its availability and food value) for game such as deer, to capture insects such as grasshoppers and wasp larvae used as food, and to drive game (including rabbits and deer). Northern Paiute Indians told anthropologist Isabel Kelly, in 1932, how groups of deer, spotted on a hilltop, were sometimes encircled with fire. "The fires were brought closer, constricting the circle until the animals were bunched on the crest on a hill where they could be shot conveniently" (Riegel et al. 2006, 225).

Plate 11. Basketry materials require straight stems, like those that emerge after burning. Lucy Parker (a Yosemite Miwok–Paiute–Kashaya Pomo–Coast Miwok) used willow stems in a twining style for this storage basket.

Plate 12. The bulb, or corm, of a brodiaea was food for native Americans and helps the plant to sprout after fires.

Burning by Indians was not uniformly applied across the state. Some landscapes were burned nearly every year, often near villages, particularly in oak woodlands and grassland prairies. The Indian population residing in Yosemite Valley exerted a strong influence over vegetation patterns in the Valley, while natural lightning ignitions probably dominated the fire regimes through most of the high-country landscape. Evidence that the population residing in Yosemite increased about 650 years ago is seen in suddenly higher charcoal levels in the soil layers. An increase in oak pollen, and a simultaneous decline in pine pollen, correlates with burning by Indians, which benefited oak trees while thinning out the pines.

Some ecosystems became anthropogenic types, dependent on burning by humans to persist. Examples include patches of grass maintained in chaparral or within redwood forests, desert fan-palm oases, coastal prairies, and oak woodlands. "Without an Indian presence, the early European explorers would have encountered a land with less spectacular wildflower displays, fewer large trees, and fewer park-like forests, and the grassland habitats that today are disappearing in such places as Mount Tamalpais and Salt Point State Park might not have existed in the first place" (Anderson 2005, 2).

Aboriginal burning ended across California as disease and warfare destroyed populations after Spanish missions were established in the late eighteenth and early nineteenth centuries. That transformation accelerated and spread across the state following the gold discovery in 1848 and was completed in the years that followed as settlers redesigned California's habitat management.

In the following decades many ranchers and sheepherders also burned to keep grasslands open for grazing by their animals. Loggers burned the forest understory and slash piles, particularly during the early decades of the twentieth century (see "The Flames of History").

Fire Behavior

Once ignited, the progress of a wildfire and its behavior are strongly influenced by weather and the landscape's topography.

Weather

Weather comprises the air pressure, temperature, humidity, precipitation, wind, and cloud conditions at any given moment. The term "climate" refers to weather over time, not just averages, but also the range of variability and extremes that characterize a location. For example, average wind speeds in southern California do not reveal the importance of periodic episodes when extremely dry, hot, Santa Ana winds howl across the coastal plain.

In most of California, the wildfire season begins in early summer, a couple of months after the last winter storms, and ends whenever winter rains begin again, generally by November or December. The state's pattern of wet winters and dry summers is characteristic of Mediterranean climates (map 3). Under that pattern, the optimum growing season comes in late winter and early spring. In summer, many plants go dormant as a zone of high pressure in the northeastern Pacific Ocean blocks the approach of storms, keeping California's weather dry. In winter, the Pacific High slides southward, opening a storm track for northern storms.

The state's wet weather usually moves in from the ocean with westerly winds. Precipitation in California is greatest in the north. The state's mountain ranges—the Coast Ranges, the Sierra Nevada, and the transverse ranges of southern California—generate heavier rain on their western slopes as they force air to rise, cool, and drop its condensed water vapor. The mountains also create rain-shadow effects as air descends to the east, grows warmer, and, thus, holds on to its moisture.

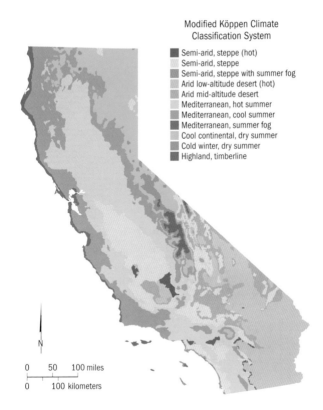

Modified Köppen Climate
Classification System

■ Semi-arid, steppe (hot)
▨ Semi-arid, steppe
▨ Semi-arid, steppe with summer fog
▨ Arid low-altitude desert (hot)
▨ Arid mid-altitude desert
□ Mediterranean, hot summer
■ Mediterranean, cool summer
■ Mediterranean, summer fog
□ Cool continental, dry summer
■ Cold winter, dry summer
■ Highland, timberline

N

```
0        50     100 miles
0              100 kilometers
```

Map 3. California climate zones.

The varied conditions that result are reflected in vegetation types and, ultimately, in different fire regimes.

How a specific fire behaves within those broad parameters is a product of wind, temperature, and humidity, factors that firefighters and prescribed-burn specialists monitor through weather forecasts and with on-site measurements. During the fire season, the burning index is calculated daily from local measurements of temperature, relative humidity, fuel moisture, wind, and precipitation. The index is used to set fire

Plate 13. A fire danger rating sign near a Bureau of Land Management fire station.

danger levels, commonly posted along highways near fire stations and ranger stations (pl. 13), and, along with air quality conditions, helps determine burn days, when it is legal to burn with a permit. The National Weather Service also issues "fire weather watches" to alert agencies that they are likely to issue a Red Flag Warning in the next 12 to 72 hours.

Wind

Wind dries out fuels by carrying moisture away, delivers oxygen to help fires ignite, and then fans the flames. Winds help preheat adjacent fuels by bending flames and moving heated air toward unburned material. High winds often loft burning embers to ignite new spot fires downwind.

Winds are named for the directions they come from: a north wind arrives out of the north, for example. Wildland firefighters learn to watch for shifting wind directions that affect fire behavior as day turns to night. The sea breeze is a west wind in California. During the day, the land heats up more quickly than the ocean. Warmer air rises and is replaced by cooler air blowing off the ocean. Land breezes reverse the flow direction in the evening, as the uplands cool more rapidly than the ocean. A similar wind-shift occurs daily on inland hillsides and mountain slopes. During the heat of the day, valley-mountain winds blow uphill, often quite powerfully, as heated slopes cause warmed air to rise. In the evening, as hill-tops and slopes cool before valleys and ravines, winds reverse direction. Cooler air sinks downward from the ridges, usually blowing more gently than the earlier upslope winds. Occasionally, stronger downslope winds, called sundowners, which drop onto the coastal plain in the evenings as the sea breeze dissipates, have been responsible for major fires near Santa Barbara.

When weather patterns produce high pressure over the Great Basin and Mojave deserts, powerful Santa Ana winds blow hot and dry across southern California's coastal basins and out to sea, often at more than 60 miles per hour. They are a special category of land breeze, most noticeable in the fall. Air moving away from the inland high pressure is funneled through mountain passes and descends to the coastal plain. Descending air is compressed by the increased weight of the atmosphere overhead, which makes it warmer (at a general rate of 5.4°F per thousand vertical feet of descent).

These Santa Anas are southern California's annual harbinger of extreme fire weather. They arrive when fuels are at their driest point in the year. It is no coincidence that the threat of wildfire peaks at the same time. While the winds blow, the moving air dominates everything and everyone in the region. Wildfires that occur during Santa Ana winds are usually not extinguished until the weather changes. The wind sends flames racing across the landscape. Hot embers sail above fuel breaks and can ignite spot fires a mile ahead of the flaming front (pl. 14). The high winds sometimes force flames even through very young, recently burned chaparral fuels.

Plate 14. Santa Ana winds can carry embers that can start new spot fires a mile ahead of the main fire.

Complicating the challenge of fire suppression, strong winds make it too dangerous to fly aircraft such as tankers and helicopters that carry water or fire retardant, just when they are most needed.

Occasionally, a similar wind pattern occurs in the San Francisco Bay Area, where it is called the Diablo wind. High pressure inland pushes air out of the Central Valley from the direction of Mount Diablo, the dominant mountain peak east of the Bay.

Very large fires can also create their own winds and local weather. The rising heat can cause water vapor to condense in pyrocumulus convection clouds, and can lift smoke and ash high into the atmosphere. In a forest fire "blow-up," where the entire forest canopy is suddenly consumed, the energy released can generate winds similar to the destructive energy of hurricanes.

Topography: Lay of the Land

Because heat rises, fires generally burn faster uphill (pl. 15). Narrow canyons or chutes may act as chimneys, feeding heat and fire upward. Flames on slopes also bend toward unburned fuel, preheating it and helping the fire spread. Houses built at the top of a slope are at an increased risk from the flames and heat climbing up the hillside. Burning debris may also roll down hills and start new spot fires.

Plate 15. Because heat rises, a tilted match burns "uphill."

The aspect of slopes, whether they face north or south, for example, can produce different exposures to sunlight or to prevailing weather systems, leading to different moisture levels in dead fuels and living vegetation. Entirely different plant communities may grow on opposite-facing slopes of the same canyon (pl. 16). Even on one hillside, differences in shade and heat will exist between canyon bottoms and ridge tops, or where rock outcroppings interrupt the terrain. Fuels are seldom uniform across the landscape; neither are fires.

Computer programs have been developed to estimate fire behavior in different vegetation types under different conditions of fuel moisture, terrain, and wind speed. In Sonoma County, for example, assuming flat terrain with a 20-mile-per-hour wind and typical late-summer fuel moisture levels, four-

Plate 16. Different microclimates produce different vegetation communities on opposing hillsides.

foot flame lengths would be expected at the head of a fire in grassland, six-foot flames in oak savanna, seven-foot flames in coastal scrub, nine-foot flames in dense conifer forests, and 18-foot flames in chaparral (fig. 3). Southern California's

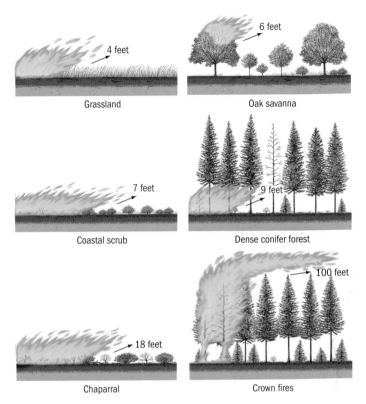

Figure 3. Flame lengths in different fuels.

denser chaparral can generate 47-foot flame lengths! Crown fires in forests (or in shrublands during extreme winds) might have 100-foot flame lengths.

How a specific fire behaves, then, is a function of its topography, particular weather conditions, and fuel types. Patches of unburned fuel often are left inside the perimeter of even severe wildfires, as are gradations between low-intensity scorching and total combustion. This range of outcomes should be kept in mind while reading the next section: a general overview of fire ecology in California's variety of plant communities.

California has always been and will continue to be a fire environment unmatched in North America.

—JAMES K. AGEE, 2006, XI

Fire Regimes

Plant communities provide the material for burning and reflect responses to fire. Though fire is often erroneously thought of as a disruption of normal conditions, it is actually a predictably regular, if episodic, ecological process. Specific fire regimes have characteristic patterns of seasonality, fire-return interval, size, spatial complexity, intensity, severity, and fire type. Those characteristics vary across the state and over time (particularly with long-term climate changes), producing variable plant and animal adaptations. Fire-adapted species are those whose survival and reproductive strategies have been shaped by the presence of fire in the environment. Species may be inhibited by or sensitive to fire. They may have adaptations that allow them to tolerate or resist fire. Some species in California are enhanced by or even dependent upon fire for their survival and successful reproduction. And some, in places where fires rarely happen, live independently of fire.

Those with life cycles most closely tied to fire have been termed pyrophytes, meaning "fire lovers." In the years immediately following burning, certain fire-follower species respond with a burst of germination that takes advantage of favorable postfire conditions. Wildflowers such as lupines, phacelias, and poppies (pl. 17) make postburn sites intensely colorful for a few brief years. They then fade back into the background, with dormant seeds waiting, invisibly, until another fire arrives. Fireweed *(Epilobium angustifolium)*(pl. 18) thrives on the reduced competition after fires in moist areas of mixed conifer forests.

Fire-return intervals describe the average time before fires reburn a given area. Where short intervals are the norm, species are under strong selective pressure to adapt. Fire-tolerant and fire-dependent species predominate in those conditions. Longer fire-return intervals generally correspond with fire-sensitive species. Some vegetation communities experience

Plate 17. Fire poppies *(Papaver californicum)* appear after chaparral fires.

Plate 18. Fireweed plants in a moist meadow.

complex combinations of both frequent light surface fires and stand-replacing crown fires at very long intervals. Specific examples are described in the section on California's vegetation types.

Intervals can sometimes be determined through historical records preserved in the annual growth rings of tree trunks, in locations where low-intensity surface fires have burned without killing trees. Researchers look for charred scars in bark and wood. Sometimes large scars, or "cat faces," are very apparent on the surface where trees were able to heal the edges of fire wounds (pl. 19), but smaller scars also lie hidden inside trunks, covered by later growth. Core samples may be taken using a hollow drill, called an increment borer. Samples may miss scars, though, so cross sections of stumps or standing trees, from sections close to the ground, are also studied to give more complete data.

Cross sections are smoothed with fine sandpaper, and then annual growth rings are counted with a microscope. The average number of years between fire scars during the life of the tree gives the mean fire-return interval (pl. 20). Records

Plate 19. A cat-face scar in the Grizzly Giant giant sequoia, in the Mariposa Grove in Yosemite National Park.

from many trees in a landscape can be cross-dated, so that researchers can distinguish large, area-wide fires from localized small fires.

Because the cells within a growth ring are larger and their

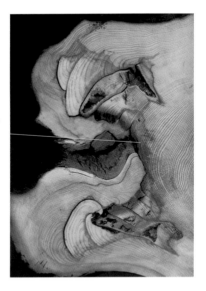

Plate 20. A cat-face scar, or cavity, was maintained in this coast redwood tree by at least seven fires spaced at seven- to 14-year intervals. A long period without fire, after burning by Sinkyone Indians stopped, then allowed bark to heal over the interior of the cat-face *(at the center of the image).* This cross section was cut from a stump of a tree logged in the 1930s and now is in Humboldt Redwoods State Park.

cell walls are thinner during the spring than later in the growing season, it is sometimes possible to tell in which season a fire occurred. The fire-scar record has been used to confirm that, for hundreds of years, most forest fires have burned in midsummer through early fall in California's Mediterranean climate zones.

Seeds, Sprouts, and "All of the Above"

Mature plants survive fires by protecting the vital tissues where growth occurs and new stems and leaves form. Buds may be wrapped in insulating scales and pitch. Bark is a protective layer of insulation that protects the cambium, where stem growth happens. In perennial plants, dormant buds capable of resprouting are insulated belowground in root crowns,

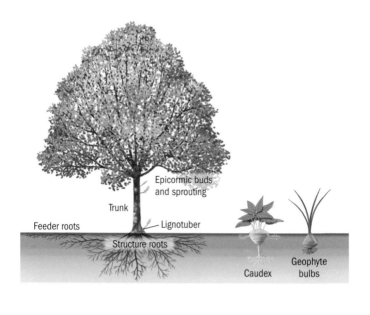

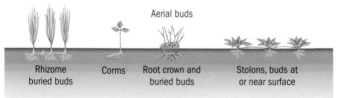

Epicormic buds
and sprouting

Trunk

Feeder roots

Lignotuber

Structure roots

Caudex

Geophyte
bulbs

Aerial buds

Rhizome
buried buds

Corms

Root crown and
buried buds

Stolons, buds at
or near surface

Figure 4. Roots and buds: the location of buds on a plant determines its response to burning.

bulbs, or underground rhizomes or may grow along the trunk and branches, high enough above the ground to be distant from flames and heat (fig. 4). The carbohydrates stored in roots and bulbs give young sprouts a start in life, while the extensive root system of the tree or shrub, still in place, easily serves a far smaller amount of new foliage. Sprouts in upper branches are elevated to take advantage of decreased competition for sunlight.

Plate 21. Whispering bells seeds germinate after exposure to smoke.

Plants can also respond with flower and seed strategies. Fires can stimulate increased flowering, the release of seeds, and germination of dormant seeds "banked" in the soil. Annual plants, unlike perennials, have meristems that are exposed as the plant grows. Instead of resprouting, their reproductive strategy must be built around seeds that regenerate after fires. Plants that have no choice but to reproduce from seeds are termed obligate seeders.

Fires improve the odds of seedling success by reducing competition, increasing exposure to sunlight, and releasing fertilizing nutrients. Heat, smoke, or chemicals in charred wood can stimulate seed germination. Heat ruptures waxy cuticles and impermeable cell layers, letting water enter and wake the "sleeping" seed. Ceanothus (*Ceanothus* spp.) shrubs may germinate from banks of seeds after over 200 years of dormancy! Whispering bells *(Emmenantha penduliflora)*(pl. 21) germinate when exposed to the nitrogen dioxide in smoke for as little as one minute.

Plate 22. Bishop pine cones remain closed and attached to limbs until the heat of a fire opens the scales and releases seeds.

When the scales on serotinous cones, gummed shut with resin, are heated by fire, the resin melts, scales open over the next few days (a delayed reaction that avoids the flaming period), and seeds are released into the wind. Temperatures high enough to melt the resin are usually between 113°F and 122°F, cool enough to not damage the seeds in the cones. Closed-cone pines do not drop cones each year but hold them on the tree limbs (pl. 22). Seeds inside these persistent cones may stay viable for decades. Serotiny is an adaptation to fire, but those trees may not be entirely fire dependent, sometimes releasing their seeds on very hot, dry summer days (see "Closed-Cone Pines and Cypresses," later in this section.)

Obligate seeders may be favored over resprouters after very high severity fires, but for long-term survival they need enough time before the *next* fire to reestablish a viable seed bank in the soil or in mature serotinous cones on branches. Where fires return too frequently, populations may not be able to persist on those sites.

Plate 23. A canyon live oak *(close)* and a coast live oak tree *(in background)* resprout after a fire.

Many perennials are obligate resprouters, obliged to resprout after their aboveground portions are consumed by fire. Obligate resprouters tend to be deeply rooted, have short-lived seeds, and grow on wetter sites than where obligate seeders dominate. Sprouting is not solely an adaptation to fire. Other events, such as floods and heavy grazing by animals, can stimulate resprouting. As anyone who has ever pulled weeds from a garden learns, unless the entire root is unearthed, many plants will sprout back.

Sprouting is not common among coniferous trees, but the coast redwood *(Sequoia sempervirens)* is an exception. Logged redwood stumps commonly grow multiple sprouts, and fallen trees serve as nursery logs, with new growth along their lengths. Charred trunks and branches can also sprout, producing a pipe-cleaner effect. Most of the state's native hardwood trees resprout. Tanoak trees *(Lithocarpus densiflorus)*, common in the Coast Ranges of central and northern California, have underground lignotubers that look like large woody potatoes and can respond with dozens of sprouts if their tree trunks are cut.

Certain other perennial plants follow a mixed strategy and can both resprout from stumps and reproduce from seeds. These facultative sprouters may be fire neutral, neither enhanced nor inhibited by fire. (In fire ecology texts, the adjective "facultative" describes the ability to live under varying conditions or options.) Oak trees that produce copious amounts of acorns but can also resprout from root crowns and elevated stems after burning are considered fire-enhanced facultative sprouters (pl. 23).

Vegetation Types and Fire

California's vegetation variety (map 4) reflects the fact that the state stretches so far, north to south, across more than seven parallels of latitude, punctuated by mountains, valleys, and desert basins that produce major variations in temperature and precipitation. Soil types also contribute to vegetation varieties. For example, chaparral shrubs are often (though not exclusively) found on serpentine soils. Though distinct classifications are identified, here, vegetation types often intermix along the boundaries of their ranges, and such categories inevitably simplify complex relationships.

Chaparral Shrublands

Chaparral shrublands (map 5) cover about seven million acres in California, more than any other vegetation type. Spanish rancheros bestowed the name "chaparral," because the thickets of brush were similar to scrub oak vegetation in Spain called *chaparro*. The vaqueros chased free-roaming cattle on horseback into nearly impenetrable thickets, so chaps were invented, the protective leather leggings worn by cowboys.

Chaparral shrubs are woody, mostly evergreen, with leaves that conserve water by being small, thick, leathery, fuzzy, and waxy. Leaves do not wilt during the dry summer and autumn

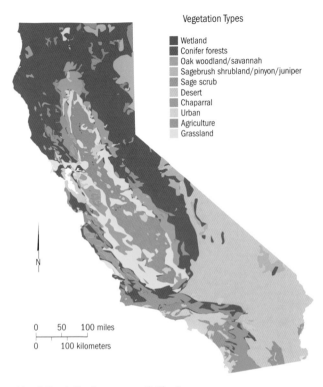

Vegetation Types

- Wetland
- Conifer forests
- Oak woodland/savannah
- Sagebrush shrubland/pinyon/juniper
- Sage scrub
- Desert
- Chaparral
- Urban
- Agriculture
- Grassland

0   50   100 miles

0   100 kilometers

Map 4. Vegetation types across California.

seasons, although growth shuts down until winter rains arrive. The dormant period coincides, of course, with the hot, dry "fire weather" season. Small leaves also increase ignitibility, as with any form of kindling, by increasing the amount of fine-fuel surfaces exposed to heat. Add in the flammability of resinous oils and gradually accumulating dead branches that are held within the brush canopy as the years go by, and chaparral becomes the most flammable vegetation type in the United States. When chaparral burns, it can seem like a hillside soaked in gasoline has been ignited (pl. 24).

Map 5. Chaparral range in California.

Plate 24. Chaparral burns during the Simi fire of October 2003, near Santa Clarita, watched by units of the CAL FIRE Nevada-Yuba-Placer Strike Team.

Adaptations to fire include reproductive responses that in many cases are enhanced by burning. Some chaparral shrubs and herbaceous plants are fire dependent. Many of the shrubs resprout from root burls. Others are obligate seeders, with seeds that may require intense heat for germination. And some take advantage of both strategies.

When chaparral burns, crown fires consume the tops of shrubs, so that a burned area regrows as vegetation stands all the same age, dating back to the last fire. Mosaics of different-aged stands give variety to landscape vistas (pl. 25). Though chaparral always burns as crown fires, flames may sometimes poke along, generating low intensities, or when pushed by wind, can race through the shrub canopy and leap forward as embers ignite spot fires. Most chaparral fires remain small, especially those ignited during early summer, but a few large autumn fires, coinciding with Santa Ana winds, account for most of the acres burned.

Fire and the state's human population are both intimately connected with chaparral. Millions of Californians live within or on the edges of chaparral shrublands, which means that millions of people live with fire. The relationship has been made famous by television coverage of flames, smoke, burning homes, and, once rains come, the floods and debris flows that often follow hillside fires (see "Soil, Water, and Air," later in this section). "Infamy" might be a better way to describe the negative opinions about chaparral generated by such publicity. The destruction of houses is obvious and telegenic; chaparral's natural attractions and biological diversity are more subtle concepts.

Fire starts have increased in lockstep with human population growth. Though more fires are ignited, most are quickly extinguished. The total annual acreage burned in chaparral

Plate 25. A mosaic of different-aged vegetation is often visible on chaparral hillsides, dating back to the last time each patch burned.

has been nearly constant, however, during the last half century (in some counties since 1910), because of periodic very large fires that overwhelm fire suppression efforts (see "The Chaparral Dilemma" in "Burning Issues").

Natural fire-return intervals average 30 to 40 years in the southern California shrublands, with some areas going unburned for 100 years and others burning much more frequently. Shortened intervals can cause type conversions, where grasses replace shrubs that have not had time to produce a bank of seeds or to replenish energy in their root systems. A positive feedback loop develops where exotic grasses, quick to burn and quick to recover with seeds, serve as fuel for increasingly frequent fires, ensuring that shrubs are eliminated and grasses favored.

In contrast to that problem, in parts of northern California, the effectiveness of fire suppression and the end of burning by Indians allowed chaparral to spread onto former grasslands. Also, in places where ponderosa pine *(Pinus ponderosa)* and California black oak *(Quercus kelloggii)* trees used to dominate, high-intensity fires have temporarily converted forest to shrublands.

The specific mix of chaparral vegetation varies around the state, so a number of naming systems have been created. Depending on the dominant shrub, there can be chamise chaparral, manzanita chaparral, ceanothus chaparral, or scrub oak chaparral. Climate zones help distinguish montane versus desert chaparral. In montane chaparral (pl. 26), some precipitation comes as snow, and shrublands grade into the understory of conifer forests.

Chamise *(Adenostoma fasciculatum)*, the state's most widespread chaparral shrub, is a facultative sprouter (pl. 27). Individual plants may survive many fires and live hundreds of years, but some mature shrubs are killed in fires, so the species broadens its chances of survival by also producing a bank of long-lived seeds that germinate after fires. Chamise may occupy the more-exposed south-facing slopes of some canyons

Plate 26. Gray pine and chamise in montane chaparral of the Sierra Nevada foothills.

Plate 27. Chamise resprouting after a fire.

across from wetter north-facing slopes where scrub oaks *(Quercus herberidifolia)* and other sprouters are more likely to grow.

The gray green of a hillside of chaparral often is temporarily replaced after fires with splashes of color from wildflowers. A number of poppy species and lupines are among the fire-followers that signal a regrowth has begun. Plants that sprout from bulbs are commonly scattered among chaparral shrubs, including soap plant *(Chlorogalum pomeridianum)* and mariposa lilies (*Calochortus* spp.)(pl. 28).

Plate 28. Splendid mariposa lilies and poppies appeared the spring following the Cedar fire of 2003 in Cuyamaca Rancho State Park.

Another class of shrubland exists in California, distinct from chaparral. Coastal sage scrub grows on low-elevation hillsides where conditions are drier than even chaparral will tolerate. Sometimes it grows on south-facing slopes, while chaparral occupies the north-facing side of a canyon. Coastal sage scrub has leaves that are softer than chaparral and often are aromatic. A distinguishing difference from chaparral appears each summer, when many shrubs in this plant community drop their leaves (pl. 29).

Plate 29. Many shrubs in the coastal sage scrub plant community drop their leaves each summer.

Coastal sage scrub often burns in the same fires as nearby chaparral, but the fire regimes have differences. Because leaves drop and shrubs go dormant, dead, dry fuels become available each fire season. Exotic annual grasses are common here, and when they dry out, more fuel is added. These annual processes mean that coastal sage scrub becomes flammable irrespective of the age of its shrub canopy and the time since the last fire. Similar adaptations to fire occur in the shrubs, however. Facultative sprouting is the approach used by species that give the vegetation community its name: California sagebrush *(Artemisia californica)*, purple sage *(Salvia leucophylla)*, and black sage *(S. mellifera)*. Laurel sumac *(Malosma laurina)* and lemonade berry *(Rhus integrifolia)* are also resprouters.

Plate 30. Gray pine cones held in the tree branches will release seeds after a fire or, sometimes, on hot days.

Some trees intermix with chaparral shrubs. One is the gray pine *(Pinus sabiniana)*(also associated with oak woodlands and sometimes called foothill pine). Massive cones protect seeds from the heat of fires, opening after that exposure, but they also open slowly over several years in the absence of fire, so the species is considered semiserotinous (pl. 30). Gray pines are so full of flammable resins, often with pitch visibly running down the trunks, that they have been called gasoline trees and will torch up through their crowns during surface fires.

Conifer Forests

Ponderosa Pine and Jeffrey Pine

Highly fire-resistant ponderosa and Jeffrey pines *(P. jeffreyi)* are part of the mixture in mixed conifer forests, along with moderately fire-resistant sugar pines *(P. lambertiana)*, fire-resistant Douglas-firs *(Pseudotsuga menziesii)*, white fir *(Abies concolor),* incense-cedar *(Calocedrus decurrens),* and extremely fire-resistant giant sequoias *(Sequoiadendron giganteum).* In such mixed forests, a mixed set of fire regimes results, with complex patterns varying from low-intensity surface fires to large, stand-replacing crown fires.

Ponderosa pines are found in all of California's mountain ranges: the Coast Range, the Klamath Mountains, the Cascade Range, throughout the Sierra Nevada, and the peninsular ranges of southern California. They are exceptionally well adapted to a regime of frequent, low-intensity surface fires. Before fire was excluded, these forests were open, often described as parklike by early observers. This is the forest type most characteristic of the light-burning debate of the early twentieth century (see "Flames of History"), because fire exclusion brought such profound changes to its fire regime.

The Jeffrey pine is closely related to the ponderosa pine (pl. 31), and the two species' ranges overlap. Pure stands of Jeffrey pines are common east of the Sierra crest.

Plate 31. The blackened base of a Jeffrey pine, which can survive low-intensity fires.

Adaptations to fire by ponderosa and Jeffrey pines include thick, corky bark that is difficult to ignite, looking like overlapping puzzle pieces (pl. 32). The lower branches of these long-lived trees drop away as the trees mature, a self-pruning adaptation that keeps limbs at a distance from the flames and heat of surface fires. Scales enclose buds, so that trees can survive even when more than half of their crowns have been scorched. Tall trees are poised to release seeds from high overhead, allowing the seeds to sail into openings created by fire.

Ponderosa and Jeffrey pine seedlings are shade intolerant. They need open space to grow and typically establish only where mineral soil has been exposed and openings have been created by fire. That results in groups of trees that are close to the same age. Scales cover the buds on seedlings as they grow, so they have some fire resistance at that early stage, but many seedlings will be eliminated by the surface fires characterizing these forests, so that old-growth trees can dominate the forest without understory competition.

Fuel to feed the frequent fires is provided by understory grasses, herbaceous plants, and fallen pine needles. Ponderosa and Jeffrey pine needles are long and, with cones and fallen chunks of resinous bark, form a loosely packed litter, full of air spaces that make it ideal as kindling. Each year, one or two tons of litter may accumulate on each acre beneath the pines. Decomposition is slow in these relatively dry forests (generally with less than 25 inches of rain each year) and is primarily a job handled by fire.

Historically, fires in ponderosa pine communities burned naturally every five to 25 years. A 600-year-old tree might survive 30 fires or more. On the west slope of the Sierra Nevada, stands of ponderosa pine sampled from the Feather River southward to the San Joaquin River drainage showed average return intervals of seven to nine years.

When domestic livestock grazing entered these forests, it reduced or eliminated grasses that had helped carry frequent, low-intensity ground fires beneath the trees. With fire exclu-

Plate 32. Ponderosa pines have thick bark and the mature trees have no branches close to the ground.

sion, shade-tolerant white firs encroach on ponderosa pine forests. The white firs, when young, are fire sensitive, and seedlings are normally controlled by surface fires. When allowed to crowd into the forest, they compete with pines for moisture and nutrients. Spindly, dense growth, with white fir branches beginning near the ground, increases the intensity of surface fires (pl. 33). As the white firs grow up toward the forest canopy, they become ladder fuels that can carry fire into the crowns, introducing a completely changed fire regime.

In the mixed conifer forests of southern California, unprecedented numbers of trees died in the 1990s, the end result of overcrowding due to fire exclusion, plus the debilitating effects of smog and drought, which weakened the trees' natural defenses against bark beetles (pl. 34). Millions of dead trees in the San Bernardino National Forest became poised to burn, threatening mountain resort communities.

Bearclover *(Chamaebatia foliolosa)*, also called mountain misery or kit-kit-dizee, commonly grows as groundcover beneath the mixed conifer forest canopy in the Sierra Nevada. It has finely divided foliage full of volatile oil that permeates

Plate 33. Harold Biswell, a University of California forestry professor and pioneer in prescribed burning, inspected the built-up fuels of a Sierra Nevada pine forest in 1966.

Plate 34. Dead trees in the San Bernardino National Forest near Lake Arrowhead.

the air; both the leaf geometry and the oil promote flammability and the frequent fires of these forests (pl. 35). Bearclover responds to fire by sprouting from rhizomes growing about eight inches below the surface, where they are protected from the heat of even very intense fires.

Plate 35. The bearclover understory being ignited during a prescribed burn.

Giant Sequoia

The giant sequoia is a truly fire-dependent species. It grows in groves in moist basins in the central and southern Sierra Nevada, remnants of a much broader range when the climate was different (map 6). Their seeds are held in serotinous cones that may remain closed for 20 years. Seeds may be liberated from young, green cones by hungry Chickarees (also called Douglas Squirrels) *(Tamiasciurus douglasi)*. The larvae of Long-horned Wood-boring Beetles *(Phymatodes nitidus),*

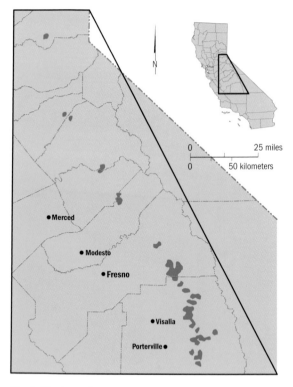

Map 6. Giant sequoia groves.

Plate 36. Fires will open the serotinous cones of giant sequoias and also provide the exposed mineral soil the seeds need to germinate.

digging through cones, can cause them to dry, shrink, and release seeds. But, most critically for this tree species, the heat from fires opens giant sequoia cones and stimulates their seeds to germinate (pl. 36).

Adaptations to a fire regime of frequent, low-intensity surface fires include extremely thick bark loaded with fire-resistant tannin. Like ponderosa pines, as giant sequoias age, the self-pruning adaptation eliminates lower limbs that might otherwise become ladder fuels. The seedling must begin its life on uncovered mineral soil to successfully take root. Seedlings do not tolerate shade, so the occasional high-severity-fire creates the openings and the sunlight exposure seedlings need. This is the only Sierra Nevada conifer that resprouts (though only when young).

Gifford Pinchot headed the Division of Forestry within the Department of Agriculture in 1899. In his journal descriptions of a tour of the West in 1891, he recorded observations about California's giant sequoias and fire:

> But who shall describe the sequoias? When the black marks of fire are sprinkled on the wonderfully deep rich ocher of the

Plate 37. *Upper:* In 1890, the "Confederate group" of giant sequoias in the Mariposa grove in Yosemite National Park. *Lower:* By 1970, white fir trees obscured all but the fire-scarred sequoia on the left. Thickets could have carried fire into the crowns to kill the sequoias. *Right:* In 2002, the scene had been restored, through thinning and burning, to a condition similar to what existed before fire protection allowed shade-tolerant firs to encroach.

bark, the effect is brilliant beyond words. These highly deco-
rative but equally undesirable fires bulked large in the minds
of the Kaweah colonists, most of whom were Eastern tender-
feet. One of them told me they had saved the Big Trees from
burning up twenty-nine times in the last five years. Which
might naturally have raised the question, who saved them
during the remaining three or four thousand years of their
age? (Pinchot 1947, 44)

Fire-scar records in giant sequoias go back more than
3,000 years. Fire-return intervals in Kings Canyon National
Park ranged from seven years on west-facing slopes to 16
years on east-facing slopes. Though high-severity fires happened in small patches, low-severity surface fires were much
more characteristic. As John Muir wrote:

> One is in no danger of being hemmed in by sequoia fires, be-
> cause they never run fast, the speeding winds flowing only
> across the treetops, leaving the deeps below calm, like the bot-
> tom of the sea. Furthermore, there is no generally distributed
> fire food in sequoia forests on which fires can move rapidly.
> Fire can only creep on the dead leaves and burrs, because they
> are solidly packed. (Muir 1878, 822)

Plate 38. Mountain whitethorn resprouting following burning near the Mariposa grove.

The greatest threat to these amazing trees comes from fire exclusion, as shade-tolerant fir trees gradually invade the groves and become ladder fuels. Fires started under those conditions could climb into the forest canopy of the giants and be intense enough to overcome all of their defenses against fire. Fire-exclusion policies that created that threat have been reversed in national and state parks with groves of giant sequoias, but the situation still had not been corrected by 2006 in some groves managed by other agencies (pl. 37).

Understory plants that are compatible with the low-intensity frequent-fire regime of giant sequoia forests may include mountain dogwood *(Cornus nuttallii)* trees and mountain whitethorn *(Ceanothus cordulatus)* shrubs (pl. 38).

Closed-Cone Pines and Cypresses

Like the giant sequoia, closed-cone pines and some cypress *(Cupressus* spp.) trees have made significant adaptations to

Plate 39. Knobcone pine cones remain closed and attached to the tree until released by fire.

fire, sometimes to the point of dependency, relying particularly on serotinous cones. Seeds are held within the cones, which remain attached to branches of the trees. The seeds are released only after heat from a fire (or, sometimes, a hot summer day) heats the resin and opens the cone scales (pl. 39).

This reproductive strategy often corresponds with a regime of stand-replacing crown fires. Typically, dead trees and fallen detritus accumulate in these forests until crown fires move through, killing standing trees but releasing a rain of seeds from the persistent cones. Seedlings will take advantage of the fertilized ashy seedbed and exposure to sunlight. Some pines produce both serotinous and nonserotinous cones to maximize their survival options. Fire exclusion can reduce the incidence of serotinous species, but at the other extreme, too-frequent fires lead to immaturity risk, if enough new cones have not been banked before the next fire arrives.

Knobcone pines *(Pinus attenuata)* are one of the best ex-

Plate 40. A Coulter pine cone and seedling after the 2003 Cedar fire in Cuyamaca Rancho State Park.

amples, as they are strongly serotinous. Knobcones grow associated with the chaparral fire regime and within mixed forests and woodlands. Without fires, knobcone pines could gradually disappear from the landscape.

Coulter pines *(P. coulteri)*, with massive, heavy cones (green cones commonly weigh five pounds)(pl. 40), are widely distributed in the central coast and southern California chaparral regions. Coulter pines vary in their serotiny, most strongly showing the closed-coned character where they grow in chaparral fire regimes that generate intense crown fires. The species is less serotinous when it associates with other woodland trees, such as coast live oaks *(Quercus agrifolia)*, where surface fires are typical.

The bishop pine *(P. muricata)* is another fire-dependent, obligate seeder. Seeds released by fire can germinate even after cones have endured temperatures up to 203°F. New cones are brown, but they gradually weather to a dusty-looking gray as the cones age on the trees. Older trees have thick bark to withstand low-intensity surface fires, but stands of bishop pine gradually grow dense until fuel buildup coincides with fire weather, leading to stand-replacement fires and even-aged groups of trees. Northern California populations are less serotinous than southern ones.

The Coast Ranges' Monterey pines *(P. radiata)* are moderately serotinous. They can open some cones every year, but most seeds are held, to be released following fires. Another coastal conifer, beach pines *(P. contorta* var. *contorta)* are, by contrast, fire neutral, growing where very long intervals occur between fires. Though cones persist for many years on trees, seed release is not dependent on fire.

Lodgepole pines *(P. c.* var. *murrayana)* have thin bark and a shallow root system, and adult trees are susceptible to fire. The species is considered only semiserotinous in California, where most lodgepoles drop seeds each year, but some serotinous cones are also produced (pl. 41). In the Sierra Nevada, lodgepoles grow at the higher-elevation zone of conifer forests, where fuels are sparse and extensive fires are infrequent. Lodgepoles reproduce well after a fire does happen, where forest stands adjacent to burned acreage provide plenty of seeds (pl. 42).

Outside of California, the species is more fully serotinous, an adaptation to conditions where stand-replacement fires occur. The massive Yellowstone fires of 1988 burned primarily through lodgepole forests adapted to very long fire-return intervals of about 300 years. In those areas, lodgepoles that die gradually generate a dead fuel load, so when drought and fire weather eventually coincide, conditions are ripe for a stand-replacement crown fire.

Eight species of cypress are native to California. Most have serotinous cones and adaptations to fire similar to the closed-cone pines. McNab cypress *(C. macnabiana)* and Sargent cypress *(C. sargentii)* are most widely distributed. Like the rarer tecate *(C. forbesii)* and Cuyamaca *(C. arizonica)* cypresses,

Plate 41. Lodgepole pine cones that have opened and released seeds without the aid of fire.

they associate with chaparral shrubs, sharing that regime of high-intensity, stand-replacement fires. They grow in dense stands, have thin bark, and have lower branches that do not self-prune and so serve as ladder fuels, and after mature trees are killed by fire, seeds are released from charred cones.

Plate 42. Lodgepole pine snags after a stand-replacing fire.

Subalpine

Above the range of lodgepole pines, up toward the tree line in the mountains, wildfires become very rare (pl. 43). Individual trees may be struck by lightning, but fuels are too patchy for fires to spread. Yosemite researchers calculated a fire rotation in whitebark pine *(Pinus albicaulis)* longer than 27,000 years! This is not a "real" number, because these subalpine forests must have come and gone and been modified as climate changes occurred over such a long period, but it makes the point that, today, fires are *extremely* rare in this environment. Other conifers in this high country are mountain hemlock *(Tsuga mertensiana)*, limber pine *(P. flexilis)* in the eastern Sierra Nevada, and foxtail pine *(P. balfouriana)* in the southern Sierra Nevada.

Coast Redwood and Douglas-fir

Coast redwoods are the tallest trees in the world. They grow in very damp forests along a narrow, foggy strip of the California

Plate 43. A scorched juniper snag in the high-country of the southern Sierra Nevada.

coast, extending 450 miles from the Oregon border down to southern Monterey County. They are fire enhanced and fit into the category of facultative resprouters: seeds are shed from cones each year, but the trees are also prodigiously good at sprouting. Seedlings do best on fresh mineral soil, like that exposed by fire, but also take advantage of openings where floods or wind storms have toppled trees. The seedlings are shade tolerant, unlike their Sierra cousins, the giant sequoias. Coast redwoods also respond to fire with abundant numbers of sprouts from their root crowns or from burls up on the blackened trunks. Fallen trees may have rows of young sprouts

Plate 44. The thick bark of a coast redwood tree may be charred after a fire but ensures the tree's survival.

spaced along their lengths. The new trees that result are genetic clones of the original. Stumps of logged trees also commonly sprout.

Fires seldom kill the big trees. Their list of adaptations includes the great height for which they are famous, which lifts branches far above surface flames. They have very thick bark made of spongy fibers and loaded with tannin, a fire-resistant chemical that also provides resistance to insects and fungi (pl. 44). Fire scars become common on old trees, hollowing out their bases or creating ledges upon the trunk where bark smoldered in long strips.

Fallen litter builds up beneath coast redwoods. Most of it decomposes under the damp conditions, but the loosely packed ground fuel, full of air spaces, can become flammable when it is dry. In the presuppression fire regime, burning consumed irregular patches of the understory fuel with occasional fires climbing into the crowns of individual trees. Ignitions by Indians were probably responsible for most of the fires in locations with short fire-return intervals. Their burning opened and maintained "prairies" in the forests to promote growth of basket materials, encourage grass with edible seeds, harvest grasshoppers, and increase food growth for deer and elk.

Considering how wet redwood forests are (they are classified as temperate rain forests), it may be surprising that understory fires occur fairly frequently, on five- to 25-year intervals. Fire regimes in coast redwood forests in the northeastern Santa Cruz Mountains have been determined by ring counts of stumps, downed logs, and live trees. The earliest recorded fire in that sample occurred in the year 1615 and the last fire in 1884. For all sites combined, the mean fire-return interval was 12 years.

The two sets of statistics—the interval range from five to 25 years and a mean of 12 years for one region—are numbers that summarize plenty of variability and complexity. In coast redwoods, the key ignition source was not relatively rare lightning, but burning by Indians that was not applied uniformly across the land. Differences in topography and exposure further complicate the characteristics of burns. Yet, for thousands of years, fires have been prevalent enough throughout the coast redwood range to forge the species' adaptations. Forest Service scientist Steve Norman feels that the key message is that "many of the humid redwood forests burned frequently, in the past, because of a long history of human influence, and many of the forest attributes that we value today resulted from those fires" (S. Norman 2006, personal communication).

The coast redwood associates with Douglas-fir through-out its range. Where conditions favor Douglas-firs over red-woods, they sometimes grow in nearly pure stands, or often in forests codominated by Pacific madrone *(Arbutus menziesii)*, and tanoak, with Douglas-firs dominating the overstory. As sites become drier, away from the influence of coastal sum-mer fog and down through the west slopes of the Sierra Ne-vada, Douglas-fir becomes part of the mixed conifer forests.

Douglas-fir is a fire enhanced, obligate seeder. Trees can live hundreds of years, starting to bear seeds when they are about 20 years old. Mature trees have thick, corky bark on both stems and roots. Their great height and branches are often concentrated 100 feet above the ground, helping pro-tect them from surface fires (pl. 45). Needles, shorter than those on pine trees, lie compactly after they fall, and the trees do not slough bark, as pines are prone to do, so surface fires are less intense beneath the firs than beneath pines. Nearly all natural stands of Douglas-fir were established in sites first cleared by fire.

California has a second species of Douglas-fir that grows only in the southern mountains and in much drier circum-stances. Named big-cone Douglas-fir *(Pseudotsuga macro-carpa)*, its cones are four to six inches long, much bigger than the two- to four-inch range of the standard Douglas-fir. Its adaptations to fire include the unusual ability, among coni-fers, of sprouting from its trunk following fire.

Beneath the canopy of redwood and Douglas-fir forests, a secondary subcanopy can be dominated by tanoak. These small trees can be hundreds of years old, capable of sprouting after fires from root lignotubers (some tubers have been un-earthed that were as big as a small car).

Sudden oak death disease, caused by the *Phytophthora ramorum* pathogen, has been killing tanoaks and other broad-leaf trees in recent years and increasing fire danger in those forests and woodlands. Over a million tanoaks, California

Plate 45. Mature Douglas-fir trees may self-prune their lowest branches, which keeps surface fires from climbing into their crowns.

black oaks, coast live oaks, California bays *(Umbellularia californica),* and madrones have succumbed to the introduced disease, especially along the central and northern coast regions of the state. Prescribed burns are being tested by researchers as a possible means of disease control. Studies have found that areas that burned within the last 50 years have far fewer cases of sudden oak death disease.

Plate 46. Oak woodlands and savanna in the Coast Ranges.

Oak Woodlands and Savannas

Several million acres of oak trees occupy woodlands (distinguished from forests by their more open canopies) and savannas (grasslands with scattered trees). They fringe the boundaries of the Central Valley and the coastal plain of southern California, and are found along the foothills of the Coast, Transverse, and Peninsular ranges and the Sierra Nevada (pl. 46).

Oak trees living in woodlands are adapted to fire regimes with frequent low-intensity surface fires. Fires were set by Indians, sometimes on an annual basis, to promote the health of the trees and their acorns, which were a key food source. Other food plants grew beneath the oaks and adapted to the local fire regime. Examples are the various types of brodiaea (*Brodiaea* spp.), sometimes called Indian potatoes, for their edible bulbs that resprout after burning. Many oaks respond to burning by sprouting from their bases, but also from branches of the scorched trees.

Though California has many old-growth oaks, seedling regeneration, particularly in the deciduous oaks (those that drop leaves each year), has become uncommon in many areas. Both grazing and urban sprawl threaten oak regeneration, but absence of summer surface fires also contributes to the problem. Acorns can require mineral soil or light duff conditions to sprout, like those found following low-intensity fires.

Eighteen species of oak (in the genus *Quercus*) grow in California, dominated by blue *(Q. douglasii)*, valley *(Q. lobata)*, coast live, interior live *(Q. wislizenii)*, California black, and Englemann *(Q. engelmannii)* oak.

Coast live oak is very fire resistant, with thick insulating bark. Engelmann and valley oaks also have thick bark. Canyon live oak *(Q. chrysolepis)*, in contrast, is fire sensitive. The trunk and branches will burn, but the trees sprout vigorously from their root crowns.

California black oak is found in mixed conifer belts. The autumn drop of black oak's large leaves generates lots of forest litter, but frequent fires, often set by Indians in the old days, previously controlled the buildup of surface fuels. Though even mature trees have thin bark and are sensitive to fire, blackened trees respond with sprouts from the base and from the trunk and branches overhead (pl. 47). Fire exclusion can lead to competition by conifers that lowers the vigor of oak trees and increases fuel loads beneath the tree to the point where black oaks can be killed by unnaturally intense fires.

Other plants associated with oak woodland include poison-oak *(Toxicodendron diversilobum)*, a vigorous resprouter whose smoke is a hazard to firefighters, redbud *(Cercis occidentalis)*, and California buckeye *(Aesculus californica)*.

Sagebrush Shrublands and Pinyon-Juniper Forests

The high-elevation deserts of the eastern Sierra Nevada and northeastern plateaus in California have very short growing

Plate 47. An oak tree resprouting after the 2003 fire in Cuyamaca Rancho State Park.

seasons, with winter snow and warm, dry conditions in the summer (pl. 48). Most of a year's growth may be confined to a few weeks from May to early July, after the likelihood of freezing is over but moisture is still available. Shrubs and trees develop deep, extensive root systems to find water. Lightning from unstable weather that most commonly arrives midsummer is the primary natural source of ignition in the region,

High fuel loads in dense sagebrush can produce flame lengths equivalent to chaparral fires (47 feet on level ground with low wind speeds). Intense crown fires occur at fairly long return intervals, though they are often patchy because fuels are not continuous. The gray green big sagebrush *(Artemisia tridentata)* dominates this scrub community, a dominance that increased in the nineteenth and twentieth centuries due to livestock grazing. Sagebrush is not easily digested by most grazing animals, so cows and sheep focus on grasses and edible shrubs in the scrub community, improving competitive

Plate 48. Sagebrush scrub and pinyon-juniper forest.

advantages for the sagebrush. It is sensitive to fire, regenerating only by seed, and can take 30 to 100 years to recover in burned areas.

Other common shrubs in the scrub community are rubber rabbitbrush *(Chrysothamnus nauseosus)*, which sprouts after fires and can also pioneer into open areas from seeds blown by desert winds, and antelope bitterbrush *(Purshia tridentata)*, which is fire sensitive and only a weak sprouter, with greater survival after spring burns than after autumn fires.

Perennial and annual grasses grow among the shrubs. Some perennial wildflower species sprout abundantly in the years after fires, including arrowleaf balsam root *(Balsamorhiza sagittata)* and desert larkspur *(Delphinium parishii)*(pl. 49).

Where heavy domestic animal grazing has reduced native annual and perennial grasses, cheatgrass *(Bromus tectorum)* moves in, shortening the fire-return interval to the point where shrublands may convert to grasslands (pl. 50). Cheat-

Plate 49. Where sagebrush shrubs were burned, arrowleaf balsamroot and larkspur flowers dominated the hillside.

grass earned that name because as soon as the annual grass flowers, its spiky seed heads become worthless to grazing animals. Another exotic annual weed sometimes common in sagebrush scrub is Russian thistle *(Salsola iberica)*, or tumbleweed.

Cheatgrass and tumbleweed increase when heavy grazing pressure depletes more edible species. They also can accelerate the return of fire and shift the fire season to earlier months,

Plate 50. When cheatgrass goes to seed and dies each year, it becomes a dry, easily ignitable fuel.

since they die in early summer but rapidly reseed after fires. Controlling these species with prescribed burns is being studied, but the timing must be just right to take out plants before they scatter seed, while not inhibiting native perennial grasses.

At higher elevations, with slightly more moisture, sagebrush scrub begins to intermingle with, then give way to single-leaf pinyon pines *(Pinus monophylla)* and Utah junipers *(Juniperus osteosperma)*. Pinyon-juniper forests, commonly abbreviated as "P-J forests," are found east of the Sierra Nevada, on the northeastern plateaus of California, and at the edge of the Mojave Desert in the Transverse Ranges, where pinyon pines associate with the California juniper *(J. californica)*.

Fire-return intervals are long, between 35 and 100 years,

or more, in the arid Great Basin habitats. The infrequent stand-replacement fires are carried between trees by understory vegetation, or move as crown fires where forest stands are dense. Pinyon pines and junipers are easily ignited and killed by fire (pl. 51). Junipers are a common, but poor, choice for landscaping yards next to wildlands, because they are very flammable. Trees recover very slowly on burned areas.

Grazing, fire exclusion, and global warming have allowed P-J forests to expand into sagebrush shrublands in the wetter parts of their range. Junipers, in particular, have been extending into sagebrush shrublands and producing dense stands, with canopies becoming continuous enough to carry crown

Plate 51.
A pinyon pine
killed by fire.

fires. Efforts to thin juniper stands, in part to preserve sage-brush habitat for species such as the Sage Grouse *(Centrocercus urophasianus)*, but also to reduce threats of wildfire to adjacent communities, have generated controversy. In the early twenty-first century, a southwestern drought led to major die-offs of P-J forests in Arizona and New Mexico. With so much loss in that part of the range, projects that limit this vegetation type in California become contentious.

Deserts

California's only native palm tree, the icon of desert oases, is the California fan palm *(Washingtonia filifera)*. Palms are fire tolerant. Their vascular bundles are scattered through the trunk mass, instead of in a ring of cambium layer just below the bark as in woody shrubs and trees, so scorching their trunks does not girdle and kill them. Other species growing at perennial desert springs are typically not as fire tolerant, so periodic fires reduce competition and benefit palms. Summer lightning is the major ignition source in the desert, but Indians burned at oases to enhance palm fruit production and clear areas for habitation (pl. 52). Ensuring that palms thrived also gave them edible flower buds and seeds, plus fronds to make baskets and sandals.

The boundaries of the Mojave Desert essentially coincide with the habitat range of the Joshua tree *(Yucca brevifolia)*, a massive member of the lily family. Joshua trees are the key to survival for many birds, mammals, lizards, and insects. Like the palms, they are monocots whose vital tissues are protected from fire within the trunks. They also can resprout.

Widely spaced vegetation in the Mojave, Colorado, and Sonoran deserts breaks up fuels and slows the spread of fires. But annual grasses and forbs that respond after particularly wet seasons can serve as fine fuels to carry fire between sparse shrubs and shorten normally long fire-return intervals. Scientists have documented a fertilizing effect from nitrogen

Plate 52. Women from the Palm Canyon Agua Caliente Reservation carry fiber bundles of California fan palm. The photo was taken before 1924.

Plate 53. Fire in the Mojave Desert in 2006.

compounds in smog. In the deserts that are downwind from California's population centers, exotic grasses such as red brome *(Bromus rubens)* and cheatgrass seem to capture the nitrogen even better than native plants. In the comparatively wet deserts of the Mojave and the sagebrush scrub region, the available moisture sustains populations of such exotic grasses. In the hotter and drier Colorado and Sonoran deserts, invasive grasses established during wet periods are more prone to population crashes during drought years.

In 2006, 65,000 acres burned in the Mojave Desert between Palm Springs and Joshua Tree National Park, ignited by lightning. The preceding winter had been very wet and generated heavy production of wildflowers and annual grasses (pl. 53).

Grasslands

Grasslands burn more often than forests and shrublands, and grasses themselves burn more readily than trees or shrubs. Grass leaves make ideal kindling because they are small and skinny, with plenty of surface area to absorb heat and dry out after the growing season. Grass can survive grazing, regular mowing, and fires because its growing points, or meristems, are at the bases of leaves. Fires typically happen during the summer and fall in California grasslands, after annual plants have put out seed and died and the tops of perennial grasses have gone dormant. The perennials will resprout from roots or rhizomes in the soil, where they are protected from heat and flames. In addition to natural ignitions, Indians burned to maintain many grassland areas that would otherwise have converted to shrubs or forest (pl. 54).

Heavy grazing that began with the Spanish and Mexican eras, spreading from the coastal basins into once sprawling grasslands of the Central Valley, helped nonnative grass

Plate 54. Grassy meadows in Yosemite valley were burned by Miwok Indians. Now the park service conducts prescribed burns to control encroaching trees and shrubs and maintain the meadows.

species invade California. Almost 99 percent of the state's original grasslands are gone, with many native grass species now endangered or threatened.

Wetlands and Riparian Woodlands

Plants that live beside rivers or in wetlands must be able to handle periodic floods. Many are vigorous resprouters, an ability that also becomes useful after fires. With roots in damp soil, this type of vegetation is usually difficult to burn, but cattails (*Typhus* spp.) and tules *(Scirpus acutus)* are annuals that die back each year, producing large amounts of dead and often dry leaves. Until the dead material decomposes, it can carry fire. Indians burned wetlands to encourage new growth in willows (*Salix* spp.), maples (*Acer* spp.), and other plants important for basketry and food (pl. 55).

Plate 55. Cattails burning near Mono Lake.

Plate 56. Aspens resprouting after a fire.

California once had five million acres of freshwater marsh and riparian woodlands. Today, it has lost 89 percent of its original wetlands and 95 percent of the riparian forests. Coastline estuaries and marshes have been covered by development. Farmers "reclaimed" most of the Central Valley's floodplain many years ago.

Along the riparian corridors in the mountains, fires help maintain stands of quaking aspen *(Populus tremuloides)*. Aspen groves produce beautiful yellow and orange leaves each fall, a color display that is punctuated, here and there, by the dark green of a conifer. Mature aspens may survive periodic fires, and younger ones will regenerate by sprouting (pl. 56). Without those fires, conifers may keep crowding in, ultimately adding enough fuel load to generate crown fires fatal to the aspens.

Alders (*Alnus* spp.), growing in many riparian zones, are a fire-neutral species with thin bark and shallow roots. They are facultative sprouters, since young trees sprout, but older trees lose the trait. Other riparian sprouters following burning include birch (*Betula* spp.) cottonwoods (*Populus* spp.), maple, elderberry (*Sambucus* spp.), and serviceberry (*Amelanchier* spp.).

Wildlife

Animals adjust to fire, responding to direct impacts from fire events and to the recovery time line set by plants. Many species simply move out of the line of fire until the burning stops and then return to take advantage of the regeneration process (pl. 57). Others go into underground burrows. Relatively few are caught and killed directly, though, in the incredibly intense fire that burned almost every acre of Cuyamaca Rancho State Park in 2003, park biologists found over 70 animals trapped in one hollow, including deer, bobcats, foxes, and birds. Radio collars showed that 10 of 11 tagged deer and four of five mountain lions survived, however.

Fires help create different habitat conditions across a landscape. Borders between different plant communities or between young and old fuels are ecological edges where resource diversity abounds. Wildlife species take advantage of those

Plate 57. A rabbit escaping from approaching flames.

opportunities. As plants reestablish in a burned area, small seed-eating mammals and birds move in. Numbers of hawks and other predatory birds commonly increase. Deer are attracted by regrowth, which can develop more protein as plants grow in the soil fertilized by ash. "Big game creatures do not eat mature trees—they feed on sun drenched browse, new grass, and lush regrowth, all of which rely on fire to rewind their biotic clocks" (Pyne 1995, 19).

Plate 58. Fire Beetles can sense the heat of a fire from miles away and fly to the fire to mate and lay their eggs while trees are still burning.

The Fire Beetle *(Melanophila acuminata)*(pl. 58) is the red-hot lover of the beetle world. It is a flat-headed wood-boring beetle that lays eggs in freshly killed trees, often as the trees are still burning. Forest trees normally deal with bark beetles by flooding them with pitch, so trees killed by fire offer a defenseless feast. It pays a beetle to reach burning trees ahead of others, because it is there it hooks up with a mate. This species has amazing sensors capable of detecting both heat and smoke from many miles away. Courtship proceeds as trees burn, until the wood is cool enough that the female can inject eggs with her ovipositor. After eggs hatch, the larvae start tunneling through the wood, helping to speed decomposition of the dead trees.

The heat-sensing mechanism is so sensitive it has been studied for military applications and to see if humans can build duplicate sensors for early detection of wildfires. Fire Beetles have been known to suddenly arrive at a fire scene and attach themselves to firefighters. Barbecues, the lights at football games, and factory smoke stacks have attracted confused

Plate 59. A Black-backed Woodpecker on a charred pine tree.

beetles. One swarm came to an oil fire in Coalinga, about 50 miles from the nearest coniferous forest, their presumed starting point.

Burned trees that remain standing provide cavities for nesting birds such as Northern Flickers *(Colaptes auratus)*, American Kestrels *(Falco sparverius)*, and Mountain Chickadees *(Poecile gambeli)*. Black-backed Woodpeckers *(Picoides arcticus)* are especially common in burned forests within their range, where they feast on beetles and other insects (pl. 59). They are joined by other predators, the hawks and owls, coyotes and bobcats, all responding to the surge in prey.

The Western Fence Lizard *(Sceloporus occidentalis)* is a resident of chaparral shrublands and so has also adapted to frequent burns (pl. 60). After a fire, the naturally dark lizards select perching sites where they will be camouflaged on blackened logs and stems. As the char gradually wears away, they spend more of their time on lighter-colored rocks.

Though endangered and threatened species are at risk of extinction, those that live in fire-prone ecosystems are often dependent on fire in the long term. Yet, a single fire event can elevate their risks by diminishing already low numbers or by isolating populations. Conducting prescribed burns in some of these habitats becomes complicated by such concerns; however, excluding fire where it shaped the evolution of plants and animals ultimately "makes the situation worse, predisposing the species and habitats to destruction by catastrophic fire" (van Wagtendonk and Fites-Kaufman 2006, 290). The Pacific Fisher *(Martes pennanti)*, American Marten *(M. americana)*, and California Spotted Owl *(Strix occidentalis occidentalis)* are species of concern living where fire is integral to the mature coniferous forests they require.

The California Gnatcatcher *(Polioptila californica)* lives in coastal sage scrub, which means the species must tolerate periodic crown fires. The Gnatcatcher's endangered status is primarily due to habitat fragmented or destroyed by urban development. An additional threat comes from fires returning too frequently, if the scrub community is converted into grassland and more of the Gnatcatcher's essential habitat is lost.

Plate 60. A Western Fence Lizard perched on a charred log, where its dark color blends with the background.

Another reptile, the Desert Tortoise *(Gopherus agassizii)* is adapted to a habitat type where fire is rare. The Mojave Desert population is listed as threatened. This species can be killed directly by fires or stressed by shifting vegetation patterns as fire regimes change. In tortoise habitat, firefighters modify standard techniques: they avoid burning out islands of habitat, check around vehicles before moving, and take special care when they travel off road.

Soil, Water, and Air

Soil, water, and air—resources that are basic to life—also have a natural range of responses to fire. Soil nutrition can be enhanced or degraded. Water quality may temporarily decline, while water runoff can increase. Where there is fire, there is smoke, which also can have both positive and negative consequences.

Because fires recycle nutrients that had been stored in vegetation, they have a fertilizing effect on soils. Nitrogen is usually the most limited soil nutrient for plants. Fires can make a flush of nitrogen available for absorption, but, on the other hand, they volatilize nitrogen, leaving less for the ground. A postfire response to drops in nitrogen levels favors the free-living bacteria that replenish nitrogen in soil. Legume species such as lupines *(Lupinus* spp.) and ceanothus *(Ceanothus* spp.) have nitrogen-fixing bacteria that live in their roots and also commonly colonize burned areas. The nutrients phosphorus and calcium are not as easily volatilized and are available to plants as ash becomes incorporated into the soil.

Dry soils are good heat insulators. During low-intensity fires, only the upper layer of duff may burn and little heat penetrates downward. Intensely hot fires can sterilize soils by burning organic matter and fungi that help promote soil health. Countering that is the fertilization effect from released nutrients, along with a rise in soil temperature—because soils darkened by fire absorb more heat—which increases soil microbe activity.

Intense fires, like those common in chaparral, sometimes increase soil water repellency. The result is a hydrophobic soil that does not absorb water well. This can happen when heat vaporizes the resins common in chaparral shrubs, which then settle onto soil particles. Like waterproofing on a jacket, repellency is temporary, and recent research suggests it has little ecological significance. The substances are slightly water soluble, and burrowing animals and growing roots gradually break apart the band in the soil where the chemicals settled. Eventually the situation returns to normal, but while the effect persists, it may increase runoff and contribute to erosion or debris flows.

Often, fires go out only when rain arrives. Heavy rains falling onto hillsides where surface vegetation and ground litter have been burned off can generate floods that are tragic for humans in those watersheds (pl. 61). On Christmas day, 2003, two months after major fires burned in the San Bernardino Mountains, torrential rains generated a 20-foot-thick flow of mud and debris that swept into a youth camp. Fifteen people died.

Postfire treatments to control erosion commonly used to rely on aerial broadcasting of nonnative grass seeds, for example, annual rye grass (Lolium multiflorum). While the need to do *something* seems imperative after a fire, to the point where land managers feel intense pressure to do seeding, and while it seems intuitive that generating roots in the top layer of bare ground should hold soil in place, often such efforts turn out to be ineffective or even make matters worse. Much of the material carried off of burned hillsides by moving water is not topsoil, but rocks and gravel that grasses cannot stop. When rain follows immediately after a fire, many applied seeds just wash away or have no holding effect, since they have not yet germinated and matured. Left alone, Cali-

Plate 61. A postfire debris flow.

fornia's fire-adapted vegetation usually begins its own rapid regeneration, and the applied grasses compete with and slow that natural recovery. Such competition from seeded grasses can actually become the goal, for example, in sagebrush scrub areas, in hopes of overwhelming cheatgrass or other exotics that invade after fires.

With these lessons learned, seeding is now preferably done using seeds from native species; however, those seeds have often not been available in large enough quantities or have not matched specific local genetic types. Cereal grains and sterile hybrids are used as alternatives because they cannot produce viable seeds and persist only through one season of growth. Widespread aerial seeding is becoming less common, with a focus on treating only the most critical sites. Rather than seeds, hydromulch and straw are sometimes applied to help hold the surface soil, but those treatments are expensive, difficult to use on large burned areas, and still carry the risk of introducing weeds.

More important than seeding, it turns out, is work done to channel drainage from roads and trails and to control off-highway vehicles on burned lands. Culverts and pipes that channel surface water need to be cleared before high water arrives. During a flood event, working in swift water to unplug culverts can be very dangerous. Warning signals for workers and anyone in the area include intense bursts of rain and suddenly muddy streams. After a recent fire, when heavy rain is falling, anyone in the watershed must stay alert, even through the night. Fatalities from debris flows have happened many times when people were sleeping. Automatic detectors are now sometimes placed in flood channels to issue early flood warnings.

Federal land management agencies are required to conduct an evaluation after a fire, viewing the situation as an emergency until any necessary rehabilitation measures have been taken. Teams focus on threats to life and property, erosion control, water quality, and loss of soil productivity.

Other effects on water include possible increases in surface water runoff, because burned plants on the watershed are using less water from the soil. Water temperatures may temporarily be elevated by the heat released during fires, and longer increases in temperature occur where streams are no longer shaded by vegetation. High temperatures reduce dissolved oxygen, a situation that can harm fish and other aquatic life. Like the effect from pulses of debris and sediments, these impacts are temporary. Streams keep flowing, flushing material away and diluting warm water, and vegetation gradually recovers to shade the area again.

Smoke may benefit plants by inducing germination of seeds or controlling fungal infections but can also be a health hazard for humans (pl. 62). (See the "Burning Issues" section for more about smoke as air pollution.)

Plate 62. Smoke near Cuyamaca Rancho State Park during the 2003 fires.

Climate Change

Carbon dioxide released by wildfires is increasingly being studied because of concerns about global warming and climate change. California's Global Warming Solutions Act became law in 2006, requiring that California's greenhouse gas emissions be reduced to 1990 levels by 2020. California's massive economy and growing population are responsible for one twelfth of the world's annual carbon dioxide emissions. Around eight percent of the state's emissions come from burning and decomposition of forests and other wildlands vegetation.

In contrast to the burning of fossil fuels, wildland fires are part of a renewable recycling process. About one quarter of the carbon dioxide put into the atmosphere each year, around the world, comes from deforestation, but about half of that is recaptured as vegetation responds to burning with regrowth, sometimes in surges that increase overall photosynthesis on the affected areas.

Major concerns exist about carbon dioxide released during fires in places such as the Amazon, where deforestation is accompanied by cycles of cutting, burning, and local desiccation that lead to even more unintentional forest fires (pl. 63). Within the United States, monitoring by scientists with the National Center for Atmospheric Research has found that carbon dioxide released by wildfires in Colorado during the 2002 fire season equaled an entire year's emissions from that state's transportation activities. Researchers there, as in California, continue to gather data to understand the effects on the overall carbon balance by determining carbon dioxide levels being reabsorbed by forests.

Although fires are affecting the climate, global warming is,

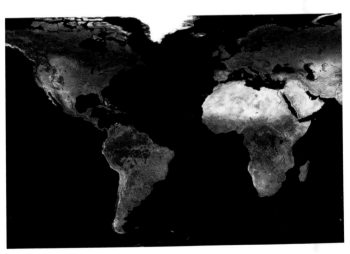

Plate 63. Fires burning across the globe between October 18 and 27, 2003.

in turn, affecting fires. Research published in 2006 suggested that warming temperatures, since 1970, have created earlier springs and longer and drier fire seasons, corresponding with increased area burned. Southwestern tree ring records going back 300 years show that most of that region's largest fires during the twentieth century came after wet El Niño winters were followed by dry La Niña drought years. The El Niño–Southern Oscillation is an ocean warming cycle that every three to seven years tends to shift heavy winter rains toward California and the southwestern states (specific effects vary enough to continue to puzzle weather forecasters). After El Niño comes La Niña, when cooler water pools in the eastern Pacific, most of California and the Southwest may dry out, and wet weather shifts toward the Pacific Northwest. As the global climate changes, El Niño events have been appearing more often.

Across the West, four times as many large, uncontrollable wildfires occurred between 1987 and 2003 as in the prior 16 years. While much of the wildfire increase in the second half of the twentieth century was related to fuel buildup in forest habitats where fire exclusion efforts had been most effective, it appears that global climate change, by magnifying the effects of weather, is now a major driving force.

Fire regimes must have always varied with the globe's natural climate. With human emissions driving global warming gases and temperature to levels not seen in the last 650,000 years, and as higher carbon dioxide levels also fertilize plant growth, creating even more fuel, land management policies will become ever more critical.

THE FLAMES OF HISTORY

In wildlands, history does repeat itself.

—JAMES K. AGEE, 2006, XIII

California's Light-Burning Debate

Federal forest reserves were established in California in 1891, administered by the General Land Office of the Department of the Interior, until the Forest Service was created in 1905 in the Department of Agriculture. Shortly after Gifford Pinchot was appointed the first chief of the new agency, he confidently declared: "Today we understand that forest fires are wholly within the control of men" (Pinchot 1910, 45). Pinchot's successor as chief forester, Henry Graves, wrote that forest fire prevention was "the fundamental obligation of the Forest Service and takes precedence over all other duties and activities" (Graves 1910, 7).

The reserves and national forests had been created to control logging, mining, and grazing practices that had been stripping the landscape across the nation. Loggers left behind slash—unmillable limbs and branches—that fueled increasingly large fires. Railroads provided a major ignition source for such tinder; locomotives that spewed cinders and sparks were the third most common cause of forest fires in 1887, after land clearing and hunters.

In California, grazing practices had also introduced unrestrained fire. In 1894, John Muir deplored the annual burning by sheep herders in the Sierra Nevada:

> Running fires are set everywhere with a view to clearing the ground of prostrate trunks, to facilitate the movements of the flocks and improve the pastures. The entire forest belt is thus swept and devastated from one extremity of the range to the other.... Indians burn off the underbrush in certain localities to facilitate deer-hunting, mountaineers and lumbermen carelessly allow their camp-fires to run, but the fires of the sheepmen, or muttoneers, form more than ninety per cent of all destructive fires that range the Sierra forests. (Muir 1961 [1894], 154)

Through the first two decades of the century, California became the center for a public debate by proponents of "light burning," who opposed the new federal fire exclusion policy. "Light burning" referred to fires purposely ignited to control growth in forests to keep the landscape open, favor certain plants over others, and reduce the threat of intense wildfires. Later, the same practices would be called "controlled burning," terminology that would be replaced with "prescribed burning" as practices were scientifically refined during the final decades of the twentieth century.

"In some quarters this method has been sneered at as 'the Digger Indian plan,'" the editor of the *San Francisco Call* wrote, on September 23, 1902, endorsing "an experienced mountaineer's" letter to the editor. "It should be sufficient compliment to this natural method that the Indian lived in, preserved, made permanent and transmitted to us on this continent the most extensive, valuable, and useful forests in the world." H. J. Ostrander's letter was titled, "How to Save the Forests by Use of Fire." He wrote: "Scientists say that in order to preserve the forests from fire, pine needles shall be allowed to accumulate, that dead brush shall not be burned out, that fallen trees shall not be disturbed. The practical mountaineer says, 'Burn and burn often, in order that this accumulation …shall not become so great as to cause the destruction of the trees when a fire sweeps through the mountains'" (Ostrander 1902, 6).

The same year, John B. Leiberg wrote a report on "Forest Conditions in the Northern Sierra Nevada, California" for the U.S. Geological Survey. He recognized fire as "the most potent factor in shaping the forests of the region.…In fact almost every phase of its condition, has been determined by the element of fire" (Leiberg 1902, 42, 44). Yet Leiberg saw that shaping force as something humanity must overcome. He felt that the land was carrying only 35 percent of the timber it could support.

In 1905, Forest Assistant E. A. Sterling with the federal Bureau of Forestry authored "Attitude of Lumbermen toward Forest Fires." Sterling identified insect damage and short-sighted lumbering methods as great problems, yet "certain...it is that fire is the greatest of forest evils" (Sterling 1905, 133)(fig. 5). He recognized that in California pine forests, fires typically burned as surface fires that "rarely destroy extensive stands of timber, although individual trees are severely injured and often killed" (135). Yet his primary concern remained the wrong-headed attitude of lumbermen who "allow [fires] to run unless they threaten their mills or are likely to spread to 'slash-ings' in dangerous proximity to valuable timber. This, too, is in the face of the fact that nothing is more noticeable in the Sierra forests than the burned-out bases of many of the finest sugar and yellow pines" (135). Sterling could not see the scars on old-growth trees as an indication that such trees survived

Figure 5. An early fire-prevention poster that demonized fire.

repeated burning during their long lives. He felt that light-burning methods left "all young growth open to destruction and *does not get at the root of the evil*" [italics added] (138). Those final words were revealing—even when used as a controlled tool, fire never was acceptable because "at the root" it was inherently the "greatest of forest evils."

Marsden Manson, San Francisco's city engineer, in a 1906 article in the *Sierra Club Bulletin,* admitted that "light fires gave open forests through which one could readily see for great distances. So impressive were these forest vistas and so majestic were the great boles that poetic and impracticable natures at once accepted the Digger Indian system of forestry as unquestionably the natural and correct one. The impression has been strengthened by...the absence of a definite knowledge of what forestry really is.... *The Digger Indian system of forestry will not give timber as a crop*" [italics added] (Manson 1906, 22, 24).

"Digger" was a derogatory term for California Indians, whose food gathering practices and "primitive" ways were scorned by the state's brash post–gold rush society. The final reference to timber "as a crop" holds the explanation for foresters who saw the "primeval" forests as damaged by forest fires (while acknowledging a historic fire regime that generated low-intensity fires). Small trees—"reproduction"—were susceptible to fire and had to be protected if the forests were to produce the maximum yield of the crop sought by "systematic forestry."

With confidence in their ability to transform the forests, war was declared on nature's fire by the young profession of American forestry. The fire-exclusion policy became firmly entrenched in the coming decades in the Forest Service and within other fire-control and land management agencies that followed the federal agency's lead (fig. 6).

Many private lumbermen and ranchers, however, continued to oppose this approach. *Sunset* magazine became a primary media outlet taking the California light-burning debate before the public. The magazine had been founded by the Southern Pacific Railroad Company to promote westward travel. Railroad land holdings, granted by the federal government, ultimately totaled 11.6 million acres within California, including large tracts of forest land.

"How Fire Helps Forestry," by G.L. Hoxie, appeared in *Sunset* in August 1910. "Practical foresters," Hoxie declared, "can demonstrate that from time immemorial fire has been the salvation and preservation of our California sugar and white pine forests. The practical invites the *aid* of fire as a *servant,* not as a *master.* It will surely be master in a very short time unless the Federal Government changes its ways" [emphasis in original] (Hoxie 1910, 145–146). Hoxie derided the "theoretical" policies of fire exclusion, worrying that if they were followed for just

> a few years longer, there will be no hope of saving these areas from useless, unnecessary and enormous damage, as the accumulated fallen limbs and unusual and unnecessary hazard is many times greater in five or ten than in two or three years. (148)
>
> Why not by practical forestry keep the supply of inflammable matter on the forest cover or carpet so limited by timely burning as to deprive even the lightning fires of sufficient fuel

Figure 6. California fire prevention notice aimed at light-burning advocates in 1913.

to in any manner put them in the position of master?...Fires to the forests are as necessary as are crematories and cemeteries to our cities and towns; this is Nature's process for removing the dead of the forest family and for bettering conditions for the living. (151)

The summer of 1910, however, was bad timing for Hoxie's argument. That year, the institutional approach to fire suppression for the young Forest Service became fixed after extremely intense fires in the northern Rockies burned three million acres in Idaho and Montana. Eighty-five people were killed, 78 of them firefighters.

William Greeley, later chief forester of the Forest Service, saw his personal experience that summer of 1910 as illuminating for "a young forester, thrown by chance into a critically responsible spot on a hot front....I had to face the bitter lessons of defeat. From that time forward, 'smoke in the woods' has been my yardstick of progress in American forestry. The conviction was burned into me that fire prevention is the No. 1 job of American foresters" (Greeley 1951, 18, 24)(pl. 64).

Like the self-perpetuating cycle of hatred that can be fueled by wartime tragedies, the dogma and emotion of righteous war against fire solidified after 1910. Fire was *the* great enemy.

The debate became even more polarized. "This theory of 'light burning' is especially prevalent in California and has cropped out to a very noticeable extent since the recent destructive fires in Idaho and Montana," the district forester for California wrote in June 1911 (Olmsted 1911, 43). F.E. Olmsted's "Fire and the Forest—the Theory of 'Light Burning'" ran in the *Sierra Club Bulletin.* Olmsted repeated the litany of arguments—fires killed "reproduction" and damaged forest qualities—but with even greater fervor and absolutism:

It is said, we should follow the *savage's* example of "burning up the woods" to a small extent in order that they may not be burnt up to a greater extent bye and bye. (43)

Plate 64. "Which is preferable...?" Photographs that accompanied W. B. Greeley's 1920 article in *The Timberman*, "'Piute Forestry' or the Fallacy of Light Burning." Greeley favored the "protected" young growth *(above)* over the "clean" forest *(below)*, "the ideal of the light burner."

This is not forestry; not conservation; it is simple destruction....The Government, first of all, must keep its lands producing timber crops indefinitely, and it is wholly impossible to do this without protecting, encouraging, and bringing to maturity *every* bit of natural young growth. (45)

> Fears of future disastrous fires...are not well founded.
> Fires in the ground litter are easily controlled and put out.
> ...Fires and young trees cannot exist together. *We must, there-*
> *fore, attempt to keep fire out absolutely* [italics added]. (46)

Rancher and novelist Stewart Edward White countered in a *Sunset* article in March 1920. "The general public, educated for twenty years by the Forest Service, reacts blindly and instinctively against any suggestion of fire. Nevertheless fire—a bad master—is an excellent servant. There are good fires and bad fires" (White 1920a, 25). White covered many points and concluded eloquently:

> One may prevent fires for five, ten, twenty-five, fifty years. But
> one cannot eliminate all carelessness, all cussedness, all natural
> causes....We are painstakingly building a fire-trap that will
> piecemeal, but in the long run completely, defeat the very aim
> of fire protection itself....Keep firmly in mind that fires have
> always been in the forests, centuries and centuries before we
> began to meddle with them. The only question that remains is
> whether, after accumulating kindling by twenty years or so of
> "protection," we can now get rid of it safely....In other words, if
> we try to burn it out now, will we not get a destructive fire? We
> have caught the bear by the tail—can we let it go? (117)

Sunset provided Chief Forester Henry Graves space in the next issue for a rebuttal titled "The Torch in the Timber: It May Save the Lumberman's Property, But It Destroys the Forests of the Future." Graves bluntly declared fire the "archenemy of the forest" (Graves 1920, 37). He reviewed familiar points: burning killed young growth and cost too much to be economical. As for White's point about fire's usefulness against insects, Graves insisted: "Fire has no such value...as a remedy for bark beetle attacks, but...even if it did, its use would not be justified" (38). To accept light burning would be "practically giving up the battle for forest perpetuation. It would mean...a disastrous sacrifice of all that we have gained in improved conditions through fifteen years of protection.... We shall not murder the patient in order to be rid of the disease" (88, 90).

In May, White explained why he was unconvinced by Graves's arguments. Then *Sunset* concluded the series in the June issue with District Forester Paul Redington's "What Is

A VERY INFLUENTIAL BEAR

World War II brought new fears of forest fires ignited by the enemy as a wartime tactic. Fire prevention and suppression became military objectives and the patriotic concern of every citizen. In 1943, the Wartime Advertising Council, seeking an iconic fire prevention sym-

bol, turned to Bambi, the deer that movie viewers had seen flee from a terrible forest fire in Walt Disney's feature movie. A year later, the National Advertising Council created Smokey, the fire prevention bear, its most successful and persistent image. Smokey has effectively shaped attitudes about fire through six decades. Today, Smokey has his own webpage at smokeybear.com. Recently, his old fire prevention message has been broadened to not only warn about "bad fire," but also educate about "good fire" and its role as "nature's house-keeper." Since 2001, Smokey's familiar "Only you can prevent..." phrase has closed, not with the words "forest fires," but with the more inclusive term, "wildfires" (fig. 7).

Figure 7. Poster from the Smokey Bear fire prevention campaign.

the Truth?" He announced the formation of a forestry committee to conclude the debate and finalize policy. In 1923, the California Forestry Committee recorded a unanimous decision in favor of the Forest Service fire-protective system. The California Board of Forestry followed up the committee report by adopting a resolution condemning the practice of light burning and favoring fire exclusion.

Though officially defeated, the burning issue simply would not go away. Nature itself would not cooperate. Inevitably, forest fuels built up as fire suppression became increasingly effective, as White and others had predicted. The bear grasped by its tail, as White described, grew bigger and more powerfully dangerous.

The goal of fire exclusion is no longer national policy. In 1968, prescribed burning began in Sequoia National Park, and that effort extended to Yosemite and other national parks in the state. California State Parks started a prescribed-burn program in 1973. The Forest Service announced its switch from "fire control" to "fire management" in 1974. The 1995 Federal Wildland Fire Management Policy and Program Review established firefighter and public safety as the top priority but also recognized fire as an integral part of wildland ecosystems. That policy was reviewed and reaffirmed in 2001. Yet, fire suppression and Smokey Bear's wildfire prevention message continue to be essential where wildland fires threaten homes and property and where natural fire regimes have not yet been restored.

The Big Ones

We are, in the end, governed by the ungovernable. By the mysterious ways of the winds. And by the ancient cycle of fire.

—ORANGE COUNTY REGISTER, 1993, 59

In the summary that follows of California's biggest fires, only the most significant wildfires are included, judged by acreage, destruction of structures, and loss of lives. Acreage statistics tell an imperfect story, because many fires burn with variable intensity and commonly leave some unburned patches as they move across the landscape. Most, but not all, of the largest and most destructive wildfires in California were products of the autumn, corresponding with extremely high winds and very dry fuels. Impacts to humans and their property increased as the decades advanced in lockstep with ever-expanding population growth, especially in southern California.

In September 1923, an early lesson about risks associated with urban areas crowding up to the edge of wildlands was delivered when fire invaded Berkeley out of the hills, driven by an east, or "Diablo," wind. Fifty city blocks with 624 structures burned.

In September 1932, the Matilija fire burned across 220,000 acres in Ventura County. That fire held the official acreage record for the next 70 years, until 2003.

In October 1933, the most deadly fire ever for California firefighters came at Griffith Park, in the city of Los Angeles. Several thousand welfare relief workers had been hired to clear brush and work on trails and roads in the park. When a fire broke out, the "unlimited manpower" nearby, armed with shovels, seemed, at first, like the ideal force to put the fire out. About 3,000 men volunteered (many later insisted they were ordered) to fight the fire. Neither the workers nor their foremen had firefighting experience. Hundreds of workers became trapped in a canyon when the wind changed direction, leaving 25 to 50 dead (the uncertainty about the number was due to poor record keeping) and 125 injured.

In July 1953, the Rattlesnake fire burned in chaparral in the Mendocino National Forest, ignited by an arsonist. The fire killed 15 firefighters following a nighttime shift in wind direction.

In November 1961, the Bel Air fire destroyed 505 structures in Los Angeles County though it burned only 6,090 acres (pl. 65).

Plate 65. Richard Nixon on his roof during the Bel Air fire of 1961.

Through most of the 1960s, there were relatively few wild-fires. In October 1967, the Paseo Grande fire, blown by Santa Ana winds, delivered flames to 48,600 acres, took out 66 homes in rural Orange County, and killed one person. That relatively insignificant wildfire, compared to others on this list, was my family's personal experience with such history. Our home, part of a horse-boarding ranch, burned while my father, older brother, a friend, and I (17 years old) protected a metal barn and ranch buildings and about 60 horses (who huddled beneath sprinklers in a large arena). We lost almost all of our personal possessions and learned how communities can pull together after such tragedies.

In September 1970, Santa Ana winds downed powerlines which ignited two conflagrations. In Los Angeles County, the Clampitt fire burned 105,200 acres and 86 structures and killed four people. In San Diego County, the Laguna fire en-compassed 175,400 acres and 382 structures and took five lives. Coordination between firefighting agencies was badly disorganized. That led to the eventual development of the Incident Command System, a standard planning hierarchy that would become familiar to all emergency personnel. Ironically, by 2003, similar problems existed because new radio technology had been developed but not widely adopted.

In July 1977, lightning ignited the Marble Cone fire which burned 177,900 acres in the Ventana Wilderness of Los Padres National Forest (Monterey County). Though the 1980s were another relatively quiet period for wildfires, lightning started several fires in August 1987 that became known as the Stanislaus Complex, affecting 146,000 acres, much of it forest, and 28 structures, and causing one death. The '49er fire of September 1988 burned 148 homes, hundreds of other structures, and 33,700 acres in the Sierra Nevada foothills of Nevada County.

In June 1990, the Painted Cave fire began near Santa Barbara during extreme fire weather: temperatures reached 109 degrees and humidity was down to nine percent. It burned only 4,900 acres but, driven by "Sundowner winds," raced toward the coast, reaching 641 structures and leading to one death.

In October 1991, Berkeley and the Oakland Hills experienced a repeat tragedy similar to the fire of 1923, but with heavier costs. Wind pushed the Tunnel fire across 1,600 acres and 2,886 structures, and that time, 25 lives were lost (pl. 66). Most who died were caught during evacuation attempts on narrow, curvy roads that became blocked by abandoned cars. Damage estimates were about $1.5 billion.

During eight days in August 1992, central Shasta County's Fountain fire burned 300 homes (a total of 636 structures) and some 64,000 acres of dense forest and brush.

October 1993 brought 14 simultaneous fires across southern California. The Kinneloa fire destroyed 151 homes in a 5,500-acre blaze. The biggest of these fires led to the "Battle of Laguna" in Orange County, with Santa Ana winds driving

Plate 66. The 1991 Oakland fire.

flames across only 16,700 acres but burning 441 structures in Laguna Beach.

In October 1999, near Redding, the Jones fire burned 954 structures and 26,200 acres. Acreage was the story on the Biscuit Complex fires of July 2002, which affected 500,000 acres, mostly in Oregon, mostly roadless or wilderness lands. Started by a cluster of 12,000 lighting strikes, the fire eventually reached into California and the Six Rivers National Forest, involving 29,000 acres of the Smith River National Recreation Area. As much as 60 percent of the acreage burned at low intensity or was unscathed within its perimeters. That same month, the McNally fire was accidentally ignited at a resort in Sequoia National Forest. It would burn uphill from shrublands into mixed coniferous forest across 150,700 acres. The McNally ended when it ran into areas that had burned in 1990 and 2000.

The year 2003 set new records for California's wildfires. Once again, 14 fires burned simultaneously across southern California, ultimately totaling 748,000 acres, 3,361 homes (and 1,100 other structures), and 24 lives taken (map 7). The most destructive of these, the Cedar fire in San Diego County, began after firefighters were already busy with eight other fires. It would involve 273,250 acres, burn 2,820 structures, and cause 15 deaths. It affected more acres and structures than any other wildland fire in the state's history (pl. 67). Started by a lost hunter who lit a signal fire, at first it barely moved away from its remote ignition site, nearly inaccessible to firefighters. Then, Santa Ana winds, out of the northeast, began blowing. The fire raced toward the coast, traveling 13 miles in just 16 hours, until the Santa Ana wind stopped and onshore winds turned the fire back through unburned fuels to the east (pl. 68). It moved out of the shrublands and into mountain timber in Cuyamaca Rancho State Park, finally stopping when it came to the boundary of a fire that had burned the year before.

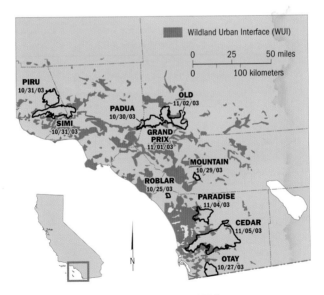

Map 7. Wildland-urban interface areas and 2003 fires.

Plate 67. CAL FIRE crews battle the Cedar fire.

At the same time, the Old fire was moving through San Bernardino County. Set by an arsonist, it would total 91,300 acres, burn 1,003 structures, and lead to six deaths (pl. 69). The Grand Prix fire began on October 21 and burned into Fontana. Its totals were 58,450 acres and 135 homes. In Ventura County, the Simi fire would burn across 108,200 acres and take 300 structures. Ten other fires were part of the regional firestorm.

July 2006 brought the Bar Complex fires, started by lightning in Trinity County and involving 100,400 acres. Then, in September, the fifth largest wildland fire in the state's history, the Day fire, affected 162,700 acres in Ventura County. Though the acreage was large, only 11 structures burned and only one of those was a home. The size of undeveloped wildland parcels involved in both of those July incidents helped keep such very large fires from becoming very large human tragedies. They provided an instructive contrast to the 2003 fires, where the tragedy was not that vegetation burned, as it

Plate 68. A line of flames approached homes in the Scripps Ranch as the Cedar fire neared the end of its westward movement. Note how wind was, at that moment, blowing smoke away from these houses, which did survive.

Plate 69. The Old fire burned out of the mountains toward San Bernardino.

eventually will, but that the fires crossed over the wildland-urban interface, destroying homes in their paths and taking many lives.

On October 26, 2006, an arsonist lit a fire in Riverside County that would be given the name Esperanza. It killed five

Plate 70. Smoke and ash blew offshore as Santa Ana winds pushed multiple fires across southern California in October 2007.

firefighters when flames overran their engine as they were trying to protect a home. Thirty-four homes were lost and over 40,000 acres were involved.

Then came 2007. Once again, October's Santa Ana winds assaulted southern California. Downed power lines, construction sparks, and arsonists ignited 23 fires (pl. 70). For more than a week, fires spread across 517,000 acres, from Ventura to south of the Mexican border. More than half a million people were ordered to evacuate. There were seven fire-related deaths and 1,969 homes were destroyed. As in 2003, San Diego County was hardest hit. Most destructive was the Witch fire, burning 198,000 acres, 1,121 homes, and 30 businesses in the north part of San Diego County.

The success of our management of the Sierra Nevada is contingent upon our ability and willingness to keep fire an integral part of these ecosystems. To not do so is to doom ourselves to failure; fire is inevitable and we can only try to manage in harmony with fire.

—JAN VAN WAGTENDONK, 2006, 290

Places developed in good faith but with a bad sense of history's blackened record: homes planted smugly in ancient fire-chutes, in places that had burned—who knows how many times?—in an ecology founded on flame.

—ORANGE COUNTY REGISTER, 1993, 9

Fighting Back:
Tactics and Weaponry

Thirty-five of California's 58 counties rely on CAL FIRE (until 2007 known as the California Department of Forestry and Fire Protection, or CDF) for wildland fire protection. CAL FIRE responds to an average of 6,300 fires that burn nearly 144,000 acres each year. The other counties have their own fire departments and, along with city and volunteer departments, handle local structure fires and make initial attacks on wildland fires. Fires on federal wildlands are fought by federally employed firefighters from the Forest Service, National Park Service, Bureau of Land Management, and other agencies. Any of these agencies may respond to calls for mutual aid when conditions require more firefighters and equipment than a jurisdiction can handle. Red, green, yellow, and white trucks may all be present. CAL FIRE plays a key role in coordinating these mutual aid forces (map 8).

CAL FIRE's most highly trained firefighters work in strike teams (sometimes called Type 1 crews) that may respond anywhere within the state. Those teams are supported by fire crews, often formed using minimum-security Department of Corrections inmates and wards from the California Youth Authority. "Hotshots" is the name given to federal firefighters who work in 20-member crews that may be sent to any state to fight fire. Their training and experience requirements exceed the standards for the state's strike team crews. The Forest Service and Bureau of Land Management also use smoke jumpers, who parachute into remote areas to make an early attack on wildfires.

During a wildfire, firefighters can be frustrated by citizens who react with questions like "Why don't they just go put it out? Spray water on it? Stop the thing?" We citizens need to understand what is actually possible when a landscape is burning. Estimated flame lengths are one way to consider firefighting options and their effectiveness and help us understand why, often, firefighters have no choice but to back away.

So long as flame lengths stay below four feet, hand crews using shovels and axes can construct fire lines near the front of the fire (pl. 71). The heat and danger from rapidly spreading fire after flames are between four and eight feet high mean that fire lines must move back a considerably greater distance; only bulldozers or other heavy equipment can clear fire lines along the fire front. Fire engines with hoses and water will

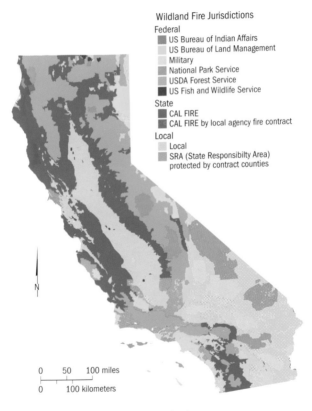

Wildland Fire Jurisdictions

Federal
US Bureau of Indian Affairs
US Bureau of Land Management
Military
National Park Service
USDA Forest Service
US Fish and Wildlife Service

State
CAL FIRE
CAL FIRE by local agency fire contract

Local
Local
SRA (State Responsibilty Area)
protected by contract counties

Map 8. Wildland fire jurisdictions in California.

Plate 71. A hand crew monitoring a backfire during the 1970 Laguna fire.

have to "knock down" such flames before crews with hand tools can approach more closely. A fire with flames between eight and 11 feet requires air tankers or helicopters to drop fire retardant to slow the fire's intensity and rate of spread (pl. 72). Beyond 11-foot flames, direct fire suppression is simply no longer effective. No amount of water or retardant can make an effective dent in the energy being released. At that point, firefighters can only work indirectly, along the heel and flanks of the fire, keeping it from spreading sideways while also moving out ahead of the advancing front (how far ahead depends on wind conditions and the distance firebrands are traveling) to make a stand where natural fuel breaks such as streams or roads are possible barriers.

A common wildland firefighting tactic is to burn out fuels between the advancing front and a new fire line. Such back-fires create a blackened zone intended to disrupt one side of the fire triangle by depriving the fire of fuel. Wildland firefighting requires different tactics than those used by city

Plate 72. A helicopter drops water during the 2006 Sawtooth fires near Palm Desert.

fire departments, where structure fires are the norm. In 2003, as the Old fire burned toward Rancho Cucamonga, hundreds of firefighters guarded the urban-wildland interface:

> The troops from the wildland side would be out in the brush performing perimeter control. Their job was to keep the fire from reaching the houses…using wildland tactics…constructing fuel breaks with dozers and conducting burn operations. Then, back right up against the houses, there would be the municipal firefighters, ready to defend the city if the fire got past perimeter control. They were not accustomed to seeing a hundred-foot wall of flame tearing toward them, and they were especially not accustomed to firefighters starting [back]fires of their own. (Krauss 2006, 79, 80)

Bulldozers can rapidly cut fire lines through heavy brush and even topple trees (pl. 73). They tear up the earth, so erosion becomes an issue where they have cut lines. The deep wounds they create can be hard to heal. Where natural resource values are paramount, other means are preferred, but when homes and lives are in jeopardy, they often become essential tools.

Aerial drops are handled by helicopters or fixed-wing airplanes (pl. 74). They may scoop or lift water in bags from nearby lakes, or else drop chemicals. Fire retardants contain wetting agents to help the material coat and adhere to vegetation and are colored red with ferric oxide to mark where they have been dropped. Some brands are designed to gradually fade to an earth tone with exposure to sun. Sulfates and phosphates in retardants can act as fertilizers to help the regrowth of plants after the fire but can be toxic to fish if dropped in water. Unfortunately, the high winds and turbulence of extreme fire weather, Santa Ana winds, or heavy smoke can make it too dangerous to fly at times when this equipment is most needed.

Plate 73. A dozer cuts a line close to the flames.

Plate 74. Air tankers drop fire retardant colored with red dye.

Firefighters can, and do, suppress about 97 percent of wildfires. On the other three percent, those that usually correspond with extreme fire weather, they fall back to indirect efforts. They will attempt to save structures if personnel, equipment, and circumstances allow. Usually only a change in weather makes firefighting efforts effective and brings the end to major wildfires.

Making Peace: Restoring Fire

Fighting fire has much in common with military warfare. Where those efforts have been most successful, to the point of temporary fire exclusion, the consequences in recent decades have been more acres burned and increasingly difficult and costly firefights. Instead of the warrior concept, some fire managers have instead become peacekeepers, aiming to restore a more benign relationship with wildland fire. Their key tool is the science of prescribed burning.

What is a prescribed burn? The term includes any fires ignited under predetermined conditions to meet management objectives, but there is more than one category (pl. 75). Besides the "front country" burns, "wildland fire use" allows naturally ignited fires to continue burning on wild landscapes, so long as they fall within the criteria—the prescription—that will accomplish specific resource goals. That somewhat bewildering term, "wildland fire use," is another name for what was, for a while, called "prescribed natural fire," and before that a "let burn." That name fell out of favor because "let

Plate 75. A prescribed burn cleaning the understory and smaller-diameter trees in a Jeffrey pine forest.

burn" sounded far too casual for something that required such stringent criteria, planning, and monitoring. In either form, the purpose of prescribed fire is to reestablish, as much as possible, fire regimes that mimic or match conditions that existed before effective fire suppression altered the condition.

Burning prescriptions look at weather, wind, season, humidity, fuel moisture, and fuel types. Plans include where the fire will travel after it is ignited and where it will either go out or be extinguished. Computer models incorporate fire behavior information with geographic information systems to predict fire spread. Smoke forecasts must be coordinated with air quality control districts. Crew safety plans and emergency procedures are specified in the planning phase. Fire breaks may be prepared to limit the burn. Equipment and personnel are organized.

Drip torches are commonly used to ignite burns (pl. 76). A match is lit and, from the nozzle of a handheld canister, burning dollops of mixed diesel and gasoline begin falling into fuel on the ground. Burning often starts at a high point at the edge of a fire line. Successive strips may be fired to burn a short distance uphill toward the cleared line, at first, and then others that burn toward the blackened zone created by earlier strips. Gradually the black zone, where fire will not carry, becomes wide enough to increase its effectiveness as a fire break. Fire can gradually creep downhill through fuels as a controlled backing fire. Dropping below that point, additional strips may be ignited as head fires that will burn uphill and join the backing fire, both going out at that point.

There are other ways to ignite fires. Terratorches are essentially flamethrowers, a way to shoot flames and extend the fire-starter's reach. Helicopters take over on large landscape-sized burns. They sometimes carry a machine that injects small balls with a chemical that starts a heat-releasing reaction inside the ball. The balls are immediately dropped from the air, and within two minutes after hitting the ground, small flames lick into the vegetation wherever a ball has landed.

Plate 76. Handheld drip torches are commonly used to ignite prescribed burns by dropping bits of flaming fuel.

Helicopters may also carry torches, slung beneath the copter, that work like giant drip torches. With helicopters, hundreds of acres can be treated in a day, so costs per acre come down.

Of almost 4,000 prescribed burns conducted by the National Park Service since 1968, one percent turned into wildfires that had to be suppressed. Similar statistics apply to the other agencies that implement burns. Some escaped fires have turned into major disasters, however. A few of the fires that burned as a complex in and around Yellowstone National Park in 1988 began as "wildland use" fires, started by lightning and allowed to burn until weather conditions changed. (Those that caused the most concern, however, were ignited by humans. A woodcutter's cigarette started the North Fork fire in the Targhee National Forest and burned into Yellowstone National Park, eventually totaling 373,000 acres.) In 2000, the Cerro Grande wildfire began after a prescribed burn in Bandelier National Park, spotted outside its boundaries. It was declared a wildfire and fought with a backfire that itself escaped control. The Cerro Grande wildfire burned into Los Alamos, New Mexico, forcing 18,000 residents to evacuate, destroying 239 homes plus 39 structures within the Los Alamos National Laboratory complex.

Investigations and national reviews of fire policy followed both those events. While measures were taken to modify techniques, both times the review panels also reaffirmed the necessity for prescribed fire to correct the problems of fire-starved ecosystems. An estimated 53 percent of forests and rangelands in the United States still have altered fire regimes as a result of fire suppression.

Air pollution concerns have become a major obstacle—perhaps the biggest obstacle—to scheduling and completion of prescribed burns, particularly in California, where air basins are already polluted with particulates and nitrogen oxide emissions from automobiles and industrial emissions. Just as agricultural burning of orchard cuttings and rice stubble has nearly been eliminated to reduce particulate pollution, regulations treat the smoke of prescribed fires as another human source of pollution. That may be shortsighted, since the smoke from intentional fires is a substitute for inevitable wildfire smoke. Through planning, much smaller smoke events can be timed to coincide with the best weather for dispersing smoke away from population centers. The massive smoke episode from major wildfires can be avoided by spreading that potential across many better-controlled smoke events (pl. 77).

Smoke from Indian burns, to sustain cultural practices, has *not* been classified as a human-made pollutant. An example of this kind of project was carried out recently in the Shasta Trinity and Six Rivers National Forests, working with the Nor-Rel-Muk Tribe of the Wintu people and the California Indian Basketweavers Association. The fuel was bear grass (*Xerophyllum tenax*), burned in the late fall, just before the first winter rain, timed to produce new shoots the next summer for quality basket materials.

Burning on private lands has been coordinated by CAL FIRE's cooperative vegetation management program since 1982. Costs are shared, and a major incentive for private property owners is that the state shoulders the liability costs. On average, 35,000 acres per year has been burned.

The Nature Conservancy is a nongovernmental organization that uses prescribed fire on their privately managed lands and teaches other private landowners to conduct burns, both nationally and internationally. It has trained more than 1,300 people in ecological fire management, from 2002 to 2004, in a program that adheres to national standards.

Some areas treated with prescribed fire have caused flames to "lie down" when they reached the treated area, helping

Plate 77. Smoke from prescribed burning is preferable to the greater release of smoke during an uncontrolled wildfire.

firefighters to stop wildfire at the edges of that location. As the 2003 Cedar fire burned back into pine forests, after winds shifted it away from the coast, its eastward spread was stopped where prescribed burning had been done on 2,000 acres during the preceding years. The effects of burning are not the same in all vegetation types, though. When southern California's Santa Ana winds blow, they sometimes move flames through very young age classes of chaparral fuel.

The Chaparral Dilemma

Because chaparral fires burn as crown fires that kill the above-ground stems, precise fire histories like those from scars in trees are not possible. Determining historic fire regimes becomes less certain. So, perhaps it is not surprising that there has been on-going debate about fire in chaparral ecosystems.

Satellite imagery and aerial photographs have been analyzed to compare 52 years of fire history north and south of the border between southern California and Baja California. Almost no fire suppression occurs in Baja when lightning or the burning done by ranchers starts fires. Ten times as many fires burned there as in southern California, but those fires were much smaller, rarely exceeding 5,000 acres. The result was a mosaic of many small fires, constrained by previously burned areas. North of the border there were fewer, but much more massive fires.

The map summarizing these data shows an abrupt transition at the international border (map 9). The pattern has been interpreted as the result of effective fire suppression in California, where most fires that start have been quickly extinguished, but because shrubland fuels then build up, eventual large fires follow.

The idea that fuel loads increase when most fires are quickly put out is intuitive and familiar, essentially the problem at the center of California's light-burning debate early in the twentieth century, and still the accepted paradigm for fire regimes such as those in ponderosa pine forests. But a different view about chaparral fire regimes has emerged among some researchers. They note that fire suppression has not excluded fire from shrublands. Essentially, the same amount of acreage has continued to burn each year—about 30 percent of the southern California chaparral landscape in every decade of the twentieth century.

While agreeing that previous fires may constrain new wildfires under moderate weather conditions, these researchers believe that the extreme force of Santa Ana winds alters the

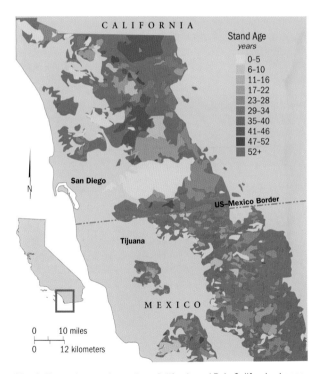

Map 9. Fire perimeters in southern California and Baja California chaparral over a 52-year period.

fuel and fire relationship. Fuel age is not irrelevant, but it is less important than severe weather and wind (map 10). Their analysis finds no statistical correlation between fuel age and fires spreading into previously burned chaparral areas. About 25 percent of chaparral fuels burn when they are less than 20 years old, and significant amounts burn in all age classes of fuel.

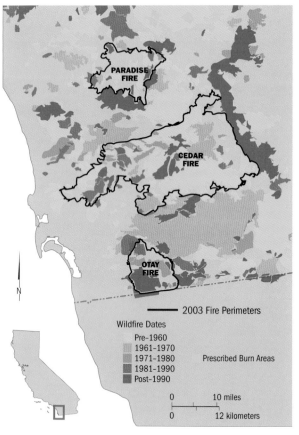

Map 10. Overlap of 2003 fire perimeters and previously burned areas.

Plate 78. A wall of flame approaches a house during the 2003 Cedar fire in San Diego County.

The other side in this debate, however, interprets the burning of young fuels during Santa Ana winds as an artifact of fire suppression: so much energy is released from the heavier fuel loads that flame fronts become too intense to be constrained by younger fuels.

These differing scientific opinions present a puzzle for land managers. Should wildland fires that start early in the season not be fought, and prescribed burning be done to create mosaics of different-aged fuels, like those in Baja California? Or should fuel-reduction efforts be limited only to the wildland-urban interface areas and places where fires are repeatedly funneled by the terrain? These researchers do agree that the fundamental problem is not that chaparral burns, but that so many people are now in the way of those fires (pl. 78).

In response to the realities of limited budgets and staffing, fuel reduction and prescribed burning projects in chaparral *are* being positioned near developed areas and other strategically valuable locations. In San Diego County, CAL FIRE has estimated that at present levels of agency capabilities, they can treat a maximum of 7,000 acres a year. At that rate, it would take 75 years before they could start the treatment cycle over again. To cut that down to about a 30- to 50-year cycle, roughly matching the fire-return interval in most of the region, they would have to burn 25,000 to 35,000 acres a year. Presently, they have little hope of obtaining the resources to meet that objective. Instead, the focus is on community protection, treating areas most at risk.

Fire Plans

Both national and California fire plans exist to assess wildland fire risks and challenges and set goals and policies. California's current plan was prepared in 1996 by the CDF and the State Board of Forestry and Fire Protection. It considers assets including wildlife, plants, ecosystems, watersheds, habitat management, public and firefighter safety, and public recreation. The California fire plan is meant to create wildfire protection zones that reduce the risks to citizens and firefighters; assess all wildlands, not just the state responsibility areas; determine who is responsible, who is responding, and who is paying for wildland fire emergencies; find ways to reduce total costs and losses, both public and private, from wildfires; and translate all of that into public policies. One of the most interesting visual resources resulting from such planning is the fire hazard risk map for each county in the state (map 11). Newly updated maps were prepared in 2007 to identify high wildfire hazard zones. Beginning in 2008, new construction in high-risk areas must meet state standards that reduce fire risk. The maps will also help owners to comply with natural hazards disclosure requirements when they sell their property.

A fire plan for the CAL FIRE Riverside unit held some surprises (fig. 8). How do fires start? In Riverside County, equipment has been by far the most common source, igniting 37 percent of fires. Children playing with fire, so often the focus

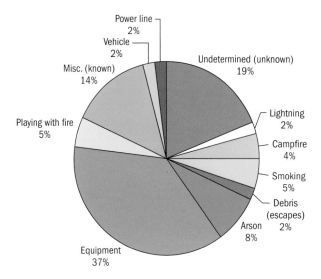

Figure 8. Sources of fire in Riverside County.

of fire prevention campaigns, started just five percent. Campfires were responsible for four percent, and lightning only two percent. A frustratingly vague 31 percent of fires were accounted for by "undetermined" (19 percent) and "miscellaneous" (14 percent) categories. Arson accounted for eight percent. It is interesting to compare these figures, which came from a developed southern California county, to data from the Six Rivers National Forest near the Oregon border. There, equipment operation figured in only six percent, escaped campfires were the big source, at 27 percent, 10 percent were caused by lightning, another 10 percent by debris burning, and arson was responsible for 17 percent,

Arsonists can act on impulse, but occasionally serial arsonists are at work. Their motives are inexplicable, particu

(text continues on page 136)

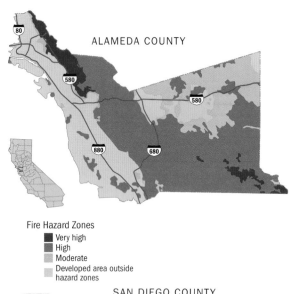

ALAMEDA COUNTY

Fire Hazard Zones
- ■ Very high
- ■ High
- ■ Moderate
- □ Developed area outside hazard zones

SAN DIEGO COUNTY

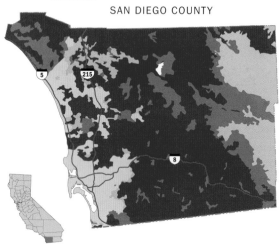

Map 11. Fire hazard severity zones.

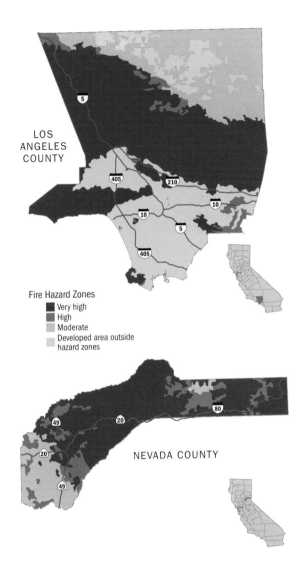

LOS
ANGELES
COUNTY

Fire Hazard Zones
- Very high
- High
- Moderate
- Developed area outside hazard zones

NEVADA COUNTY

larly to people who suffer losses because of their actions. Joseph Wambaugh, the author of many fiction stories, also has written a nonfiction account of one arsonist who set dozens of fires in California. "The serial arsonist, like other violent serial offenders, was conscienceless, egocentric, manipulative, cunning, and indifferent to societal rules and restrictions, with a compulsive need for excitement. In short, his was the classic psychopathic personality, with a unique component: the fire. Only the fire could temporarily satisfy the lust for power and control and possession. Only the flames could provide the irresistible thrill, the indescribable reward. The fire" (Wambaugh 2002, 143).

Logging versus Thinning

Whenever fire and fuel management plans are debated, a heated controversy emerges over timber harvesting, or "logging," as a way to reduce forest fuels, and whether standing dead trees should be "salvaged" after fires, before they fall and decompose (fig. 9). Removing fuel from the forest seems, intuitively, like it should reduce the threat of fire. Harvesting projects, whether they remove green trees or dead trees after fires, create jobs and bring income to local economies. But logging and thinning procedures, before or after fires, can increase a forest's flammability when slash from treetops is left behind. In the *Summary of the Sierra Nevada Ecosystem Project Report,* scientists reported to Congress that historically, "timber harvest, through its effects on forest structure, local microclimate, and fuels accumulation, has increased fire severity more than any other recent human activity. However, logging can serve as a tool to help reduce fire hazard when slash is adequately treated and treatments are maintained" (Wildland Resources Center 1996, 4).

Research done after the Biscuit fire of 2002 allowed researchers to compare fire impacts on areas that had never

Figure 9. Boondocks cartoon.

been thinned, areas where thinning was done without follow-up burning, and areas where prescribed fires were carried out after thinning. Tree mortality was highest in thinned plots where limbs and debris were left in place (80 to 100 percent). The slash burned with killing heat. Fewer trees died in the untreated stands (53 to 54 percent). Impacts were least severe where thinning had been followed by burn treatments (just five percent mortality).

Considerable controversy developed over another Biscuit fire study that concluded that areas where postfire salvage logging occurred had 71 percent fewer conifer seedlings than unlogged areas. This study also detected an elevated fire risk because of increased surface fuel loads after salvage logging. National attention became focused, not so much on the findings that salvage logging activity reduced conifer recovery, but on a request made to the journal *Science* by several university professors and some Forest Service colleagues to delay publication until a critical response could be included.

Much less controversy exists about the fact that hundreds or even thousands of trees now occupy forest acres that before fire exclusion had generally supported less than a hundred trees per acre. A return to earlier conditions would be beneficial, because such crowding stresses trees to the point that devastating crown fires occur. The Teakettle Experiment was an eight-year study in the Sierra Nevada that evaluated the effectiveness of prescribed burns, thinning, and a combination of thinning followed by burning, for ecosystem restoration in mixed conifer forests. The results showed that fire suppression is the most damaging practice to forest health. Prescribed fires after understory thinning best restored a wide range of ecosystem processes. Too much thinning, especially when cutting large overstory trees, was detrimental to wildlife.

Additional evidence that a combination of thinning and burning can improve the health of trees themselves comes from places such as the Inyo National Forest. To gradually return the Jeffrey pine forest to pre-fire-exclusion conditions of less than 30 trees per acre, thinning began in the early 1970s. The first round brought tree numbers down to 150 to 200 per acre. Twenty years later, a second round of thinning began, aiming at 70 to 100 trees per acre. Trees that were taken out were generally less than 20 inches in diameter. Slash was burned in piles or with low-intensity broadcast burns. By the early 1990s, the crews were removing trees in areas that had never been logged that averaged just seven or eight inches in diameter. But, where thinning had been done 20 years earlier, the average size removed had increased to 15 inches. After thinning, trees left behind had grown faster because of less competition for water, nutrients, and sunlight.

Tree trunks hauled away represent lost biomass that a fire would instead recycle in place. The most limiting nutrient in forests is nitrogen, with most of that stored in needles rather than in the boles, but ash does also contribute phosphorus and calcium. Burning on site also provides the benefits of heat and smoke, which trigger biological responses that are lost when fuels are reduced simply by logging. And fires move with variable effects that lead to ecosystem diversity for soils, plants, and animals.

To make thinning projects on public lands profitable for timber contractors in the Sierra Nevada forests, current policy allows removal of one tree per acre that is up to 30 inches in diameter and would not otherwise be removed. The value of that one large tree generally covers the average cost of $600

Plate 79. Thinning piles being burned in Stanislaus National Forest.

per acre to clean up slash. Without that incentive, foresters say, thinning projects might not proceed at all.

Harvests of marketable timber have always focused on tree trunks—the biggest, least-flammable vegetation in a forest. New mills and markets have gradually transitioned to work with smaller-diameter trees. In California, few can now handle trees more than 30 inches in diameter. The recent mandates to reduce California's overall greenhouse gas emissions should encourage development of more power plants that can generate electricity by burning renewable biomass, providing a market for even more small material to replace traditional fossil fuel generation.

Wherever fuels treatments and restoration efforts are considered, some general principles can be applied:

- Limited resources mean that choices must be prioritized. Such triage points to wildland-urban interface areas as the first priority.

- Mixed conifer forests are a high priority for restoration because their natural fire regimes have been so transformed by fire exclusion. Mechanical thinning of small trees and shade-tolerant species such as white fir and incense-cedar should be followed by burning of slash and downed material to reduce fuel loads, to enable the ultimate return of low-intensity surface fires (pl. 79).
- Presettlement conditions continue to be useful standards, though with global climate change, it may be impossible or inappropriate to revert back to the same conditions as a century ago.
- Every decision about fire must be specific to the site—its vegetation, wildlife, watershed characteristics, and land ownership constraints.
- Quick fixes will not meet the need for long-term landscape management.

Living in fire country today is like having a grizzly bear hibernate in your backyard; it's a thrill, but at some point the bear wakes up.

—JOHN MACLEAN, 2004, 3

MOST OF THE AREAS BURNED in the 2003 and 2007 fires were chaparral (only a small percentage was coniferous forests). This has been a familiar story in southern California when Santa Ana winds blow. The strong winds were able to push flames even into some areas that had burned as recently as three or four years earlier. The winter before the 2007 fires was exceptionally dry, producing dieback in chaparral stands and extremely low fuel moisture levels. The two prior winters, though, had been very wet, making for large crops of annual herbaceous growth to serve as fine flashy fuels. Wrapping it all together were the regional winds that howled down from the mountains, across the chaparral shrublands, then carried flames and embers into suburban enclaves.

Flammability, fuel loads, and winds do not explain the number of simultaneous fires, the number of houses destroyed, or the number of deaths in 2003 and 2007. That explanation lies with the human population. By 2003, over 18 million people resided in southern California's coastal basins, from Ventura south to San Diego.

Wildland-Urban Interface

Many of those millions live in the wildland-urban interface (WUI), the areas where structures and other human development meet undeveloped wildlands and their flammable vegetation. The state fire plan defines three levels of risk in the interface zone (map 12). Developed WUI areas are the classic interface areas, places where housing density is greater than one house per five acres, with wildlands within one mile. About nine million acres (nine percent of the state) are classified as flammable developed fire environments (pl. 80). The mixed interface zone includes areas where scattered houses are interspersed with vegetation. Mixed interface comprises over 46 million acres in California. More than 35 million acres of these (35 percent of the state) are potentially flammable mixed interface. Undeveloped WUI areas have less than one house per 160 acres in places more than three miles from any area with greater density. These areas are where ecosystem management can happen, where historic fire regimes may have created a shifting mosaic of forest structure, and the fire agencies have a reasonable chance of containing an escaped fire. This category amounts to nearly 40 million acres, or 40 percent of the state.

It pays to have fire insurance when you live in the WUI. But many of the homeowners who suffered total losses in the 2003 southern California wildfires discovered that they were

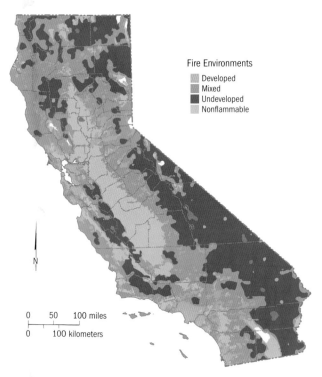

Map 12. California's wildland-urban interface areas.

Plate 80. Flames approaching Emerald Bay homes during the 1993 Laguna Beach fire.

underinsured. According to the California Department of Insurance, 2,734 total-loss claims were filed with insurers, and 22 percent—or 676—of those generated complaints to the department. Nearly half of the complaints involved underinsurance. One lesson about insurance, then, is to pay attention to coverage details, particularly about replacement after total loss and inflation adjustments to your home's value.

Representatives of the insurance industry say it costs them about $1.09 to insure homes in California's WUI for each dollar they receive in premiums. They continue in business because urban dwellers subsidize wildland homeowners through servicewide rating schedules. For those Californians who live outside the WUI, as for the rest of the nation's taxpayers who shoulder some of the FEMA disaster relief burden that so often serves Californians, financial questions arise about policies that keep permitting development on the edge of the state's wild areas.

Zoning laws to control urban sprawl may be particularly controversial in California, where so much of the economy has been driven by real estate development ever since statehood. Local governments could change building codes to mandate fire-safe construction methods, but developers fear higher costs and often oppose such measures. Multiple jurisdictions in a region may have different building codes and zoning laws that complicate regional planning. One measure that new developments ought to incorporate is green space, for example, golf courses and recreation parks, positioned as fuel-break buffers between development and flammable wildlands. Tax credits have been suggested for individuals who make investments to reduce their property's risks from wildfire.

Becoming a Fire-Adapted Californian

Could your house survive *without* firefighter protection, on its own? Do you know the fire-return interval in your area and where you fall in that regime? When was the last wildland fire to impact your neighborhood? Fires are a natural occurrence, but they become human-made disasters when we place people in their path. The government has responsibilities, but those of us who live in that wildland-urban interface also have a personal responsibility. If we handle those challenges the right way, we too can become a fire-adapted species.

Fire-Safe Planning: Before the Fire

Be prepared before a fire approaches. Construction choices for structures are as important as changes to vegetation around houses. Roofs are the first concern (pl. 81). Houses need protection from direct flames and radiated heat, of course, but blowing embers may be the most insidious source of house ignitions. Embers landing on wood shingles have been a major

Plate 81. In 1993, fire ultimately consumed this house, starting with the roof.

cause of home loss in wildfires. Class A, fire-resistant roof materials include clay and concrete tiles, metal roofing, and asphalt composition shingles. Anything less protective in the WUI zone is a mistake. Wood shakes treated with fire retardant are Class B coverings but can meet the Class A rating if underlying gypsum panels are used for additional protection. Untreated wood shakes are just inviting a roof fire (pl. 82).

Another roof issue is attic vents, which must be screened (no more than one-fourth-inch mesh) to keep flying embers out of the attic. Overhanging eaves should be boxed in. Edge gutters should be nonflammable and kept clean of debris.

Many houses have been lost when glass windows failed in the face of intense radiated heat. Double- or triple-pane windows help insulate against such loss, but installing metal shutters or preparing precut covers, to be screwed or nailed in place when a fire approaches, offers more protection. Thinning vegetation back 100 feet can eliminate most of this threat to windows.

Plate 82. Wood shingles and dry pine needles—a recipe for a roof fire.

The choice of materials for exterior walls is also important. Noncombustible choices may even lower your fire insurance bill (pl. 83). Places where embers can settle at the base of walls or in corner niches are special areas of concern. The space beneath decks and porches will accumulate embers and ignite the overhead planks (pl. 84). Decks should either be on the ground or have their overhang area protected from blowing embers with sidewalls or fine wire mesh.

Residential fire sprinkler systems are available for homes. They have the advantage of working when no one is home and could stop a domestic house fire from spreading onto neighboring land. Another level of security can be delivered with gel foams. Similar to those used by fire departments, they are sold to homeowners in gallon jugs and with spray nozzles to attach to a garden hose (pl. 85). So long as there is enough water pressure, they can coat eaves, windows, decks, wood shingle roofs, propane tanks, and even ornamental plants with a fire-resistant gel that will last for 6 to 8 hours. Later, you

Plate 83. Good construction to resist fire: a metal roof, enclosed eaves, fire-resistant walls, and decks on the ground.

Plate 84. Close vegetation and an unenclosed deck make a home harder to defend against fire.

Plate 85. Barricade gel being applied with a garden hose, one of the products available to coat a home before evacuation.

can wash away the water-soluble, biodegradable foam. If your water supply comes from your own well, consider a backup generator, so the pump can keep operating when a fire has interfered with electrical service, and, if possible, a water tank or cistern that can simply allow water to flow downhill.

Defensible Space

The objective of defensible space is to reduce the impact of fires and maximize the survivability of your home so it has the best odds of withstanding wildfire, on its own, without firefighter protection. The goals are lean, clean, and green:

- *Lean.* Break up contiguous fuels and eliminate ladder fuels by clearing space between plants, controlling the heights of shrubs, and pruning the lower limbs of trees.
- *Green.* Keep plants robust and well irrigated so they have

good moisture content. This may include substituting certain plants with less-flammable alternatives.
- *Clean.* Remove the most flammable materials: the debris of fallen leaves and branches and dead material held in shrubs and trees.

The most effective efforts change with the distance from a structure (fig. 10, table 1). In the first 30 feet, almost everything should be fireproof. Landscaping should be low, green, and regularly watered. Firewood stacks must be outside this 30-foot zone; a cord of dry firewood stacked more conveniently close is like piling 160 gallons of gasoline up against your house. That is not a wise idea when the flames and embers arrive.

From 30 feet to 100 feet (or greater distances, depending on slopes and local winds), plants should be thinned, cleared of dead material, and regularly watered (perhaps 15 minutes a week in native vegetation) so fuel moisture levels are high. Waiting to hose down plants (or roofs) as a fire approaches may be ineffective and may not even be possible, should water pressure fail. During a wildfire, electrical pumps may stop working or water pressure fall because nearby hydrants are open or because all your neighbors are spraying their roofs. A wiser alternative is to water plants on a regular basis.

Weedy grasses that are easily ignited and carry fire to larger plants should be removed or kept mowed. But do not go nude, go thin (as the San Diego County Fire Safe Council suggests). Landscapes need not and should not be entirely cleared. Removing natural shrubs and replacing them with grass can be a mistake. Not only is the grass easy to ignite, but it will not control erosion after a fire as well as the extensive root systems of native shrubs. Ice plant, grown as ground cover on many southern California coastal slopes, resists burning but is also a poor choice for erosion control. With very shallow roots, the mats of vegetation may slip when the weight of the plants builds up. Slopes not only increase the

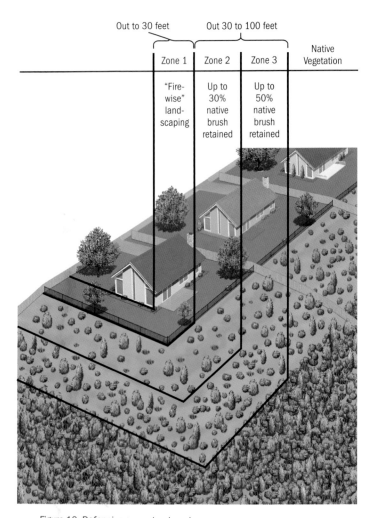

Figure 10. Defensive space treatment zones.

The labels within the figure read:

Out to 30 feet — Zone 1: "Firewise" landscaping

Out 30 to 100 feet — Zone 2: Up to 30% native brush retained; Zone 3: Up to 50% native brush retained

Native Vegetation

TABLE 1   Defensible Space Factor Study from the 1990 Painted Cave Fire, Santa Barbara

	Characteristics of Site	Surviving Structures
Wood roof	Less than 30 feet of defensible space, no defensive action taken	4%
	Less than 30 feet of defensible space	15%
Non-wood roof	More than 30 feet of defensible space	90%
	More than 30 feet of defensible space, defensive action taken	99%

Source: Adapted from Foote et al. 1991.

threat of fires burning uphill but also accelerate the velocity of water moving downslope. Erosion control needs to be balanced with vegetation choices.

Though specific actions will vary with your circumstances, these measures are legal requirements. California's Public Resources Code Section 4291 directs homeowners who live near flammable wildland landscapes to create firebreaks by clearing flammable vegetation or combustible growth within 30 feet of structures, or to property lines, whichever is less. Homeowners may be required to create additional fire protection or fire breaks within 100 feet of a structure (if ordered by local agencies on larger parcels).

The law does not mandate clearing to bare ground around residences or wholesale clearance of low-growing native shrubs and trees. Within the treated 30-foot and 100-foot zones, it allows for individual trees or other plants, including native ones, that are well pruned and maintained so that they will not rapidly transmit fire. Beyond 30 feet from a structure, grass and other vegetation may be grown to stabilize soils and prevent erosion. Shrubs should be pruned to less than 18 inches high.

You are not required to manage your neighbors' vegetation. You may be required to assent to larger fire breaks or fire-protection zones by your insurance carriers, but the insurance carrier cannot require owners to *clear* all vegetation. If your structure is built from nonflammable exterior materials, you may be allowed to modify or eliminate these fire-break and fire-protection zones, after exterior and interior inspections and the approval of local officials.

Your initial steps to establish defensible space may be the most difficult, with ongoing maintenance becoming easier. Since plants increase in size each growing season and, portions of them regularly die, having defensible space is a never-ending same-time-next-year story. Good maintenance is a necessary task that may save property and lives and, of course, is a legal requirement.

The interior of a house needs attention, also. A complete household inventory should be prepared to make insurance claims provable in case of a loss. It should include lists for every room in the house, plus the garage and outbuildings, with the value for items and serial numbers for any items that have them. A photographic or narrated videotape record can go along with the inventory list. Place a copy in a fireproof box or, better yet, store it off the premises in a bank safe-deposit box or with a relative. Also include receipts and insurance documents to support an insurance claim. The California Department of Insurance will provide a free home inventory guide to take you step by step through this process.

Before a fire, you should develop an evacuation plan and make sure all family members understand available routes to follow when evacuating and where the family should meet, if separated. Have each family member practice operating the manual lever to your electric garage-door opener, so that the door can be lifted by hand. Learn where the shutoff valve is on your propane tank or natural gas meter. A lever or handle should be easy to operate, but the time to learn how is before a fire approaches. Prepare precut covers for large ground-level windows and glass doors.

Plate 86. Horses were evacuated as flames approached during the Cedar fire of 2003.

How and where to evacuate animals, particularly large livestock, needs to be part of the plan. Horse corrals can serve as areas of bare soil where animals might be safe, depending on their size, nearby trees, and the intensity of the fire (pl. 86). Community fire-safe plans should include information about where to temporarily stable livestock. The facilities at county fairgrounds have been opened in some cases. Early evacuation can be critical to avoid animals becoming so panicked that they cannot be loaded into trailers.

Fire-Safe Planning: During the Fire

You have seen smoke. Ash may be falling from the sky. Perhaps you have been alerted by neighbors or over the phone or directly by officials. A wildfire is burning that may threaten your home. Tune in to a local radio station and listen for instructions (though rapid changes may happen and stations may not always have current, accurate information). It is time to make decisions and share them with a family member or friend. It is time to carry out the following suggested actions

that can help firefighters protect your property after you evacuate. These suggestions also apply if you are not contacted in
time to evacuate and must stay with your home.

During a wildfire, you may be advised to evacuate, to protect you and your family from life-threatening situations.
Evacuation orders may be voluntary, issued as a precaution,
or mandatory, denoting an immediate threat. The California
Penal Code authorizes officers to close areas where a menace
to public health or safety exists. It is a misdemeanor to remain
after receiving a mandatory evacuation order.

Evacuation itself can be dangerous. If you must evacuate,
do it early. Waiting too long can make traveling more dangerous than staying in place. During the Oakland Hills fire of
1991, roads became blocked, and people died when flames
ran over their cars or caught them on foot after they abandoned their trapped cars. During the Paradise fire of 2003,
deaths occurred when evacuating cars crashed, blocking the
way for cars behind them. In both fires, fire trucks were un-
able to access areas because of cars blocking roads.

Homeowners will be allowed to stay on their properties
only if their activities do not hinder firefighting efforts. Someone present to put out small fires has saved houses in neigh-
borhoods where most others have been lost. *It is critical to understand that sheltering in place is dangerous and a feasible
option only if you have properly prepared your house, your landscape, and yourself ahead of time.*

Things to Do Outdoors

Move vehicles into the garage, pointing outward, with windows
rolled up. If a vehicle must be left outside, park it away from
your house and downwind. Cars outside are prone to burn,
even if the windows are rolled up to keep embers away from the
flammable fabrics inside, because burning embers can blow
underneath and ignite the rubber tires or oily undercarriage.

Close the garage door, but leave it unlocked, ready to be
opened manually. Garages are typically full of flammable

clutter so *do not* open the door unless you are ready to drive away. Gather valuable papers and mementos and place them in a car in the garage.

Bring combustible patio furniture indoors. Shut off propane at the tank or natural gas at the meter. Prop a ladder against the house or, if it is likely to fall in high winds, lay it nearby for access to your roof. Connect garden hoses to faucets and attach spray nozzles. If you have them, nail or screw covers onto large ground-level windows and glass doors. Fill trash cans with water and put them where they will be seen by firefighters; position buckets near the swimming pool or hot tub.

Keep checking the roof and attic for embers, smoke, or fire. Consider keeping your roof moist by spraying water. Put a lawn sprinkler on the roof if water pressure is adequate. But do not waste water; you do not want to lower water pressure going to neighborhood hydrants.

Things to Do Indoors

Close all exterior doors, windows, and vents, but do not lock doors. Intense heat radiating from burning yard vegetation can ignite curtains or furniture inside a window, so take down lightweight and/or non-fire-resistant curtains and move combustible furnishings (couches, stuffed chairs, etc.) toward the center of the room. If available, close fire-resistant drapes or blinds.

Fill bathtubs, sinks, and buckets with water. Keep in mind that the water heater and toilet tanks are available sources of water. Gather rags, towels, small rugs, or mops to soak with water for beating out embers or small fires, plus any home fire extinguishers.

Go room to room, closing all interior doors and leaving a light on in each room. Lights can help firefighters locate a house at night or in heavy smoke. Turn off pilot flames to gas water heaters and gas ranges. Whether evacuating or not, you should change into cotton or wool clothing (fabrics like nylon can melt), including long pants and a long-sleeved shirt or jacket. Put on boots and gloves, a handkerchief or a painter's mask to cover your face (for breathing smoky air), prepare containers of drinking water, and carry a cell phone.

If you are there when the actual fire front arrives, move indoors and wait until it passes by (this may take a quarter of an hour or longer). As conditions improve, check outside for embers or small fires that may have started. If a fire should occur *within* the house, contact the fire department immediately.

It may seem ludicrous advice to stay calm, but it is critically important. Panic that results in foolish, last-minute evacuation attempts, for example, could be tragic. If you find yourself in this most challenging of circumstances, trust your preparations and the fire resistance built into well-designed, well-prepared homes.

What to Do after the Fire

When you return to your home after the threat of fire has ended, be alert for downed power lines, and check propane tanks and lines before turning the gas back on. Prepare your property, soon, to divert runoff that may cause floods or mudslides after the first heavy rainfall. As explained in the "Soil, Water, and Air" section, seeding to control postfire flooding may be ineffective and even slow recovery on burned land.

Kindling Change

You are not alone. In 2006, California had 160 fire safe councils. Fifty-seven of these community-based groups were in San Diego County alone. Volunteers with councils may schedule inspections to help homeowners identify their problem areas and help them make corrections. They often coordinate central drop-off locations for pruned material and cuttings to be piled, chipped, hauled away, or burned in place at no cost to the homeowner (pl. 87). Fire safe councils receive funding through donations and federal grants.

Plate 87. The community of Wawona provides a central burn pile for yard cuttings.

Population growth keeps fueling California's wildfire challenge. Someday, soon, we must resolve that issue, as it drives many of the state's environmental and quality of life challenges. Meanwhile, it is important to foster education about fire ecology concepts and the environment, to be informed citizens, aware of our places in the natural landscape, and to be leery of headlines that shout "Destruction!" and "Devastation!" wherever wildland fires have burned. The terms may apply to homes when fires cross into developed zones but are generally misleading about the effects of fire on the burned land itself.

"To eliminate fire…is to eliminate the artist's palette that provides the colors and textures of the landscape" (Wuerthner 2006, 142). That's very true, though eliminating fire is not really possible. It can only be postponed.

Fire is a transforming "artist," a creative force that forges growth and recovery by, paradoxically, first breaking things apart. Life in California must adapt to fire.

And that includes us.

ONLINE FIRE RESOURCES

Fire Prevention and Preparation

California Fire Hazard Severity Zone maps,
    http://firecenter.berkeley.edu/fhsz/
California Fire Safe Councils, www.firesafecouncil.org/
Fire prevention and safety tips,
    www.firesafety.gov/directory/public/
Firewise, www.firewise.org/
Smokey Bear program, www.smokeybear.com

California Agencies

CAL FIRE (formerly CDF), www.fire.ca.gov
California Department of Insurance, www.insurance.ca.gov
Office of the State Fire Marshal, http://osfm.fire.ca.gov

National Agencies

Bureau of Indian Affairs, Fire and Aviation Management,
    www.bianifc.org
Bureau of Land Management, Office of Fire and Aviation,
    www.fire.blm.gov
National Fire News, www.nifc.gov/fire_info/nfn.htm
National Interagency Fire Center, www.nifc.gov/fireinfo/nfn.htl
National Park Service, Fire and Aviation Management,
    www.nps.gov/fire
Sequoia–Kings Canyon National Parks Fire Information Cache,
    www.nps.gov/archive/seki/fire/indxfire.htm
U.S. Department of Agriculture, Forest Service, www.fs.fed.us/fire
U.S. Fire Administration (Homeland Security), www.usfa.fema.gov
U.S. Fish and Wildlife Service, Fire Management,
    http://fire.r9.fws.gov

GLOSSARY

Backburn A fire deliberately ignited in advance of a wildfire front to deprive it of fuel. Also called *backfire.*

Cat-face An open fire scar at the base of a tree.

Combustion Another name for fire; a rapid oxidation process chemically combining hydrocarbons with oxygen to produce carbon dioxide, water, and energy as heat and light.

Conduction The transfer of heat from molecule to molecule.

Contain a fire To complete a fuel line around the perimeter of a fire.

Control a fire To completely extinguish a fire.

Convection The movement of heat through the air.

Crown fire A fire burning in the canopies of trees or shrubs.

Defensible space An area where flammable material has been cleared, reduced, or replaced with less-flammable material, as a barrier to approaching wildland fires.

Duff The layer of soil with partially decomposed and extensively decayed organic matter, immediately above the mineral soil.

Fine fuels Fuels such as grass and pine needles that ignite readily and are consumed rapidly when dry.

Fire intensity The heat release per unit of length of fire line.

Fire line A barrier to stop the movement of fire, often formed by scraping vegetation away, down to mineral soil.

Fire regime The characteristic fire patterns of an ecosystem, including seasonality, fire-return interval, size, spatial complexity, intensity, severity, and fire type.

Fire-return interval The length of time between fires in a particular area.

Flame length The average maximum length along the axis of a flame; directly relates to fire intensity.

Fuel Any combustible material, including vegetation, such as grass, leaves, ground litter, plants, shrubs, and trees, that feeds a fire.

Fuel management Manipulating fuels to reduce the likelihood of ignition, reduce fire behavior, and/or lessen potential damage and resistance to control.

Fuel moisture The quantity of moisture in fuel expressed as a percentage of the total dry weight.

Ground fire A fire that burns in the soil layer or thick duff.

Ladder fuels Fuels that connect and can carry fire from the ground into the crown of a forest or shrubland.

Litter The top layer of intact, recognizable plant debris on a forest floor.

Oxidation The chemical union of a substance with oxygen.

Prescribed fire A fire ignited under predetermined conditions to meet management objectives. Also called *prescribed burn.*

Pyrophyte Literally "fire lover"; a species that depends on fire to survive and regenerate.

Radiation Energy (heat or light) sent as rays through the air.

Relative humidity The ratio of the moisture in the air to the maximum amount of moisture the air would hold if saturated for a given temperature.

Serotinous cones Cones that remain attached to the tree and closed until heat stimulates the cone scales to open and release seeds.

Spot fire A fire ignited beyond the perimeter of the main fire by flying sparks or embers.

Stand-replacement fire A fire that kills all of the aboveground portion of shrubs and/or trees in an area so that the stand must be replaced by new growth.

Surface fire A fire that travels through dead and down woody materials, grasses, and shrubs.

Wildfire A landscape fire started naturally or by humans, subject to suppression. Compare to *prescribed fire/burn.*

Wildland fire use Allowing naturally ignited wildland fires to burn to accomplish specific resource management goals.

Wildland-urban interface The area where structures and other human development meet undeveloped wildlands and their fuels.

REFERENCES

Agee, J. K. 1993. *Fire ecology of Pacific Northwest forests.* Washington, DC: Island Press.

———. 2006. Foreword. In *Fire in California ecosystems,* ed. N.G. Sugihara, J.W. van Wagtendonk, J. Fites-Kaufman, K.E. Shaffer, and A.E. Thode. Berkeley: University of California Press.

Agee, J. K., and C. N. Skinner. 2005. Basic principles of forest fuel reduction treatments. *Forest Ecology and Management* 211:83–96.

Anderson, M. K. 2005. *Tending the wild: Native American knowledge and management of California's natural resources.* Berkeley: University of California Press.

Aristotle. 350 B.C. *On generation and corruption,* Book 2, trans. H.H. Joachim. http://classics.mit.edu/Aristotle/gener_corr.2.ii.html (accessed October 6, 2007).

Arno, S. F., and S. Allison-Bunnell. 2002. *Flames in our forest: Disaster or renewal?* Covelo, CA: Island Press.

Baird, B. N. 2006. Comment on "Post wildfire logging hinders regeneration and increases fire risk." *Science* 313 (5787): 615.

Baker, G. M., and T.W. Swetnam, eds. 2002. *Fire and climatic change in temperate ecosystems of the western Americas.* Ecological Studies, Vol. 160. New York: Springer.

Beyers, J. L. 2003. Postfire seeding for erosion control: Effectiveness and impacts on native plant communities. *Conservation Biology* 18:947–956.

Biswell, H. 1980. Fire ecology: Past, present, and future. Keynote talk presented at the American Association for the Advancement of Science conference, Ecology Section, Davis, Calif., June 23, 1980. Manuscript of speech in Harold Biswell papers held at the Bancroft Library, University of California, Berkeley (BANC MSS 2002/67 c).

———. 1999. *Prescribed burning in California wildlands vegetation management.* Berkeley: University of California Press.

Boyd, R., ed. 1999. *Indians, fire, and the land in the Pacific Northwest.* Corvallis: Oregon State University Press.

Brown, R. T., J. K. Agee, and J. F. Franklin. 2004. Forest restoration and fire: Principles in the context of place. *Conservation Biology* 18:903–912.

Cahill, B. 2004. Cuyamaca Rancho State Park burns. *CSPRA Wave, Journal of the California State Park Rangers Association* 4 (1): 7.

California Department of Fish and Game. 2003. *Atlas of the biodiversity of California.* Sacramento: California Resources Agency.

California Department of Forestry and Fire Protection. 2004. California fire plan. http://cdfdata.fire.ca.gov/fire_er/fpp_planning_cafireplan (accessed February 22, 2007).

———. 2005. 2005 Riverside unit pre-fire management plan. http://cdfdata.fire.ca.gov/pub/fireplan/fpupload/fpppdf395.pdf (accessed February 22, 2007).

Caprio, A. C., and T. W. Swetnam. 1995. Historic fire regimes along an elevational gradient on the west slope of the Sierra Nevada, California. In *Proceedings: Symposium on Fire in Wilderness and Park Management,* tech. coord. J. K. Brown, R. W. Mutch, C. W. Spoon, and R. H. Wakimoto, 173–179. USDA Forest Service Gen. Tech. Rep. INT- GTR-320. Ogden, UT: U.S. Department of Agriculture, Forest Service, Intermountain Research Station.

Carle, D. 2002. *Burning questions: America's fight with nature's fire.* Westport, CT: Praeger.

Cottrell, W. H., Jr. 1989. *The book of fire.* Missoula, MT: Mountain Press Publishing.

Donato, D. C., J. B. Fontaine, J. L. Campbell, W. D. Robinson, J. B. Kauffman, and B. E. Law. 2006. Post-wildfire logging hinders regeneration and increases fire risk. *Science* 311 (5759): 352.

Feer, F. 2000. *Evacuating Topanga: Risks, choices, and responsibilities.* Topanga, CA: Topanga Coalition for Emergency Preparedness.

Finney, M. A., and R. E. Martin. 1989. Fire history in a *Sequoia sempervirens* forest at Salt Point State Park, California. *Canadian Journal of Forest Research* 19:1451–1457.

Fire Safe Sonoma. 2006. Living with fire in Sonoma County: A guide for the homeowner. www.firesafesonoma.org/living_with_fire.htm (accessed February 20, 2007).

Foote, E. I. D., R. E. Martin, and J. K. Gilless. 1991. The defensible space factor study: A survey instrument for post-fire structure loss analysis. In *Proceedings of the 11th Conference on Fire and Forest Meteorology,* April 16–19, 1991, Missoula, Montana, ed. P.L. Andrews and D.F. Potts, 66–73. Publication 91–04. Bethesda, MD: Society of American Foresters.

Franklin, J., L.A. Spears-Lebrun, D.H. Deutschman, and K. Marsden. 2006. Impact of a high-intensity fire on mixed evergreen and mixed conifer forests in the Peninsular Ranges of southern California, USA. *Forest Ecology and Management* 235:18–29.

Goforth, B.R., and R.A. Minnich. 2007. Evidence, exaggeration, and error in historical accounts of chaparral wildfires in California. *Ecological Applications* 17:779–790.

Graves, H.S. 1910. *Protection of forests from fire.* U.S. Department of Agriculture, Forest Service Bulletin 82. Washington, DC: Government Printing Office.

———. 1920. The torch in the timber: It may save the lumberman's property, but it destroys the forests of the future. *Sunset, the Pacific Monthly* 44 (April): 37–40, 80, 82, 84, 86, 88, 90.

Greeley, W.B. 1951. *Forests and men.* Garden City, NY: Doubleday and Co.

Gruell, G.E. 2001. *Fire in Sierra Nevada forests: A photographic interpretation of ecological change since 1849.* Missoula, MT: Mountain Press Publishing.

Halsey, R.W. 2005. *Fire, chaparral, and survival in southern California.* San Diego: Sunbelt Publications.

Harrell, R.D., and W.C. Teie. 2001. *Will your home survive? A winner or loser? A guide to help you improve the odds against wildland fire!* Rescue, CA: Deer Valley Press.

Higley, T. 2006. Personal communication to author about effects of Inyo National Forest thinning projects.

Hoxie, G.L. 1910. How fire helps forestry: The practical vs. the federal government's theoretical ideas. *Sunset* 34 (August): 145–151.

Kattelmann, R. 1999. Proposed fire management strategies and potential hydrologic effects in the Sierra Nevada. In *Science into policy: Water in the public realm,* ed. E. Kendy, 43–48. Herndon, VA: American Water Resources Association.

Keeley, J.E., and C.J. Fotheringham. 2001a. Historic fire regime in southern California shrublands. *Conservation Biology* 15:1536–1548.

———. 2001b. History and management of crown fire ecosystems: A summary and response. *Conservation Biology* 15:1561–1567.

———. 2003. Impact of past, present, and future fire regimes on

North American Mediterranean shrublands. In *Fire and climatic change in temperate ecosystems of the western Americas,* ed. T. T. Veblen, W. L. Baker, G. Montenegro, and T. W. Swetnam, 218–262. New York: Springer.

Keeley, J. E., C. D. Allen, J. Betancourt, G. W. Chong, C. J. Fotheringham, and H. D. Safford. 2006. A 21st century perspective on postfire seeding. *Journal of Forestry* 104 (2): 103, 104.

Keeley, J. E., C. J. Fotheringham, and M. Morais. 1999. Reexamining fire suppression impacts on brushland fire regimes. *Science* 284 (5421): 1829–1832.

Keeley, J. E., C. J. Fotheringham, and M. A. Moritz. 2004. Lessons from the October 2003 wildfires in southern California. *Journal of Forestry* 102 (7): 26–31.

Kent, D. 2005. *Firescaping: Creating fire-resistant landscapes, gardens, and properties in California's diverse environments.* Berkeley, CA: Wilderness Press.

Krauss, E. 2006. *Wall of flame: The heroic battle to save southern California.* Hoboken, NJ: John Wiley and Sons.

Leiberg, J. B. 1902. *Forest conditions in the northern Sierra Nevada, California.* U.S. Department of Interior, U.S. Geological Survey, Professional Paper No. 8. Washington, DC: Government Printing Office.

Lillywhite, H. B., G. Friedman, and N. Ford. 1977. Color matching and perch selection by lizards in recently burned chaparral. *Copeia* 1:115–121.

Maclean, J. N. 2004. *Fire and ashes: On the front lines battling wildfires.* New York: Henry Holt and Co.

Maclean, N. 1992. *Young men and fire.* Chicago: University of Chicago Press.

Manson, M. 1906. The effect of the partial suppression of annual forest fires in the Sierra Nevada Mountains. *Sierra Club Bulletin* 34 (January): 22–24.

Millar, C. I., and W. Wolfenden. 1999. The role of climate change in interpreting historical variability. *Ecological Applications* 9:1207–1216.

Minnich, R. A. 1983. Fire mosaics in southern California and northern Baja California. *Science* 219 (March): 1287–1294.

———. 1998. Landscapes, land-use and fire policy: Where do large fires come from? In *Large forest fires,* ed. J. M. Moreno, 133–158. Leiden, the Netherlands: Backhuys Publishers.

————. 2001. An integrated model of two fire regimes. *Conservation Biology* 15:1549–1553.

Minnich, R. A., and Y. H. Chou. 1997. Wildland fire patch dynamics in the chaparral of southern California and northern Baja California. *International Journal of Wildland Fire* 7 (3): 221–248.

Moritz, M. A., J. E. Keeley, E. A. Johnson, and A. A. Schaffner. 2004. Testing a basic assumption of shrubland fire management: How important is fuel age? *Frontiers in Ecology and the Environment* 2:67–72.

Muir, J. 1878. The Sequoia forests of California. *Harpers New Monthly* 57 (November): 813–828. http://cdl.library.cornell.edu/cgi-bin/moa/sgml/moa-idx?notisid = ABK4014–0057–115 (accessed February 20, 2007).

————. 1961 [1894]. *The mountains of California.* New York: American Museum of Natural History and Doubleday.

National Center for Atmospheric Research. 2004. NCAR aircraft, ground instruments to track carbon dioxide uptake along Colorado's drought-plagued front range. University Corporation for Atmospheric Research press release, April 26, 2004. Boulder, CO. www.ucar.edu/communications/newsreleases/2004/acme.html (accessed January 4, 2007).

National Wildfire Coordinating Group. 1994. *Introduction to wildland fire behavior, S-190, student workbook NFES 1860.* Boise, ID: National Interagency Fire Center.

Norman, S. 2006. Forest Service research ecologist, Redwood Sciences Laboratory, Arcata, CA. Personal communication to author regarding coast redwood fire adaptations. February 22.

North, M. 2007. *The Teakettle Experiment: Fire and forest health.* Davis, CA: Sierra Nevada Research Center. Interactive DVD available by request at http://teakettle.davis.edu.

Olmsted, F. E. 1911. Fire and the forest—the theory of "light burning." *Sierra Club Bulletin* 8 (January): 42–47.

Orange County Register. 1993. *Inferno! The devastating firestorms of October 1993.* Kansas City, MO: Andrews and McMeel.

Ostrander, H. J. 1902. How to save the forests by use of fire. Letter to the editor. *San Francisco Call,* September 23.

Pinchot, G. 1899. The relation of forests and forest fires. *National Geographic* 10:393–403.

————. 1910. *The fight for conservation.* New York: Doubleday, Page, and Co.

———. 1947. *Breaking new ground*. Reprinted 1998. Washington, DC: Island Press.

Pyne, S. J. 1984. *Introduction to wildland fire*. New York: John Wiley and Sons.

———. 1995. *World fire: The culture of fire on earth*. New York: Henry Holt and Co.

———. 1997 [1982]. *Fire in America: A cultural history of wildland and rural fire*. Seattle: University of Washington Press.

———. 2001. *Fire: A brief history*. Seattle: University of Washington Press.

Quinn, R. D., and S. C. Keeley. 2006. *Introduction to California chaparral*. Berkeley: University of California Press.

Radeloff, V. C., R. B. Hammer, S. I. Stewart, J. S. Fried, S. S. Holcomb, and J. F. McKeefry. 2005. The wildland urban interface in the United States. *Ecological Applications* 15:799–805.

Raymond, C. L., and D. L. Peterson. 2005. Fuel treatments alter the effects of wildfire in a mixed-evergreen forest, Oregon, USA. *Canadian Journal of Forest Research* 35 (12): 2981–2995.

Redington, Paul G. 1920. What is the truth? Conclusion of the light-burning controversy. *Sunset, the Pacific Monthly* 44 (June): 56–58.

Riegel, G. M., R. F. Miller, C. N. Skinner, and S. E. Smith. 2006. Northeastern Plateaus bioregion. In *Fire in California ecosystems*, ed. N. G. Sugihara, J. W. van Wagtendonk, J. A. Fites-Kaufman, K. E. Shaffer, and A. E. Thode, Chapter 11. Berkeley: University of California Press.

Stephens, S. L., and D. L. Fry. 2005. Fire history in coast redwood stands in the northeastern Santa Cruz Mountains, California. *Fire Ecology* 1 (1). www.cnr.berkeley.edu/stephens-lab/Publications/Steophens&Fry_2005.pdf (accessed October 31, 2007).

Sterling, E. A. 1905. Attitude of lumbermen toward forest fires. In *Yearbook of the United States Department of Agriculture, 1904*, 133–140. Washington, DC: Government Printing Office.

Stewart, O. C., H. T. Lewis, and M. K. Anderson. 2002. *Forgotten fires: Native Americans and the transient wilderness*. Oklahoma City: University of Oklahoma Press.

Sugihara, N. G., J. W. van Wagtendonk, J. A. Fites-Kaufman, K. E. Shaffer, and A. E. Thode, eds. 2006. *Fire in California ecosystems*. Berkeley: University of California Press.

Sullivan, M. 1993. *Firestorm! The story of the 1991 East Bay fire in Berkeley*. Berkeley, CA: City of Berkeley.

Swetnam, T. W., and C. H. Baisan. 2003. Tree-ring reconstructions of fire and climate history in the Sierra Nevada and Southwestern United States. In *Fire and climate in temperate ecosystems of the western Americas,* ed. T.T. Veblen, W.L. Baker, G. Montenegro, and T.W. Swetnam, 158–195. New York: Springer-Verlag.

U.S. Department of Agriculture, Forest Service. 1990. Giant sequoia. In *Silvics of North America.* Vol. 1. *Conifers.* www.na.fs.fed.us/pubs/silvics_manual/Volume_1/sequoiadendron/giganteum.htm.

————. 2000. *Living with fire.* Albuquerque, NM: USDA Forest Service, Southwestern Region.

————. 2004. Sierra Nevada forest plan amendment. Final supplemental environmental impact statement. RS-MB-046. www.fs.fed.us/r5/snfpa/final-seis/ (accessed March 2, 2007).

U.S. General Accounting Office. 1999. *Western national forests: A cohesive strategy is needed to address catastrophic wildfire threats.* GAO-RCED-99-65. Washington, DC: GAO.

Vale, T.R., ed. 2002. *Fire, native peoples, and the natural landscape.* Covelo, CA: Island Press.

van Wagtendonk, J.W., and D. Cayan. 2007. Temporal and spatial distribution of lightning strikes in California in relationship to large-scale weather patterns. *Fire Ecology* (in press). www.fireecology.net/pages/13 (accessed October 31, 2007).

van Wagtendonk, J.W., and J.A. Fites-Kaufman. 2006. Sierra Nevada bioregion. In *Fire in California ecosystems,* ed. N.G. Sugihara, J.W. van Wagtendonk, J. Fites-Kaufman, K.E. Shaffer, and A.E. Thode, Chap. 12. Berkeley: University of California Press.

Wambaugh, J. 2002. *Fire lover: A true story.* New York: William Morrow.

Westerling, A.L., H.G. Hidalgo, D.R. Cayan, and T.W. Swetnam. 2006. Warming and earlier spring increases western U.S. Forest wildfire activity. *Science* 313 (August 18): 940–943. doi:10.1126/science.1128834.

Whelan, R.J. 1995. *The ecology of fire.* Cambridge, MA: Cambridge University Press.

White, S.E. 1920a. Woodsmen, spare those trees! Our forests are threatened; a plea for protection. *Sunset, the Pacific Monthly* 44 (March): 23–26, 108–117.

————. 1920b. Getting at the truth: Is the Forest Service really trying to lay bare the facts of the light-burning theory? *Sunset, the Pacific Monthly* 44 (May): 62, 80–82.

Wildland Resources Center. 1996. *Status of the Sierra Nevada: Summary of the Sierra Nevada ecosystem project report.* Wildland Resources Center Report No. 39. Davis: University of California, Centers for Water and Wildland Resources. http://ceres.ca.gov/snep/pubs/web/PDF/exec_sum.pdf (accessed January 25, 2007).

Wuerthner, G., ed. 2006. *Wild fire: A century of failed forest policy.* Sausalito, CA: Foundation for Deep Ecology and Island Press.

Yeats, W. B. 1921. The second coming. In *The collected poems of W. B. Yeats,* 187. New York: Collier Books, 1983.

ART CREDITS

Plates

Those plates not credited below were taken by the author.

AMES RESEARCH CENTER, NASA 1, 66

JOHN AZIZ 76

MICHAEL BENARD 27, 60, and part opener (pp. 26–27)

KEITH BURSON, South Placer Fire District 24

CAL FIRE 34

RYAN CARLE 44, 45, author's photo

MICHAEL CHARTERS 12, 17, 18, 21, 39

CHRIS DOOLITTLE 69

EARTH SCIENCES AND IMAGE ANALYSIS LABORATORY, NASA Johnson Space Center 63, 70

FOREST HISTORY SOCIETY, Durham, NC, courtesy of 64

DAN GOULDNER, Barricade Gel, Inc. 85

ALLAN GRANT 65

PETE HEIN, Fuels Officer, Inyo National Forest 35, 74, 75

RICK KATTELMANN 4, 5, 42, 43, 56, 61, 87

SCOT MARTIN, California State Parks 62

NATIONAL ANTHROPOLOGICAL ARCHIVES, NAA INV 01516100, NEG 57078, Smithsonian Institute, courtesy of 52

STEVE NORMAN, USFS/PSW Redwoods Sciences Laboratory 20

ORANGE COUNTY REGISTER, courtesy of Daniel A. Anderson 81, Bruce Chambers 80, Bruce Strong (title page, pp. ii–iii), Dave Yoder 14, 71

PRESS-ENTERPRISE, courtesy of Ramon Mena Owens 2, Jose Omar Omelas 53, Jay Calderon 72

SAN DIEGO UNION-TRIBUNE/ZUMA PRESS, courtesy of Jim Baird 73, John Gastaldo 78, John Gibbins 68, Tom Theobold 57, Dan Trevan 6, 86

RANDY SCALES, CDF Firefighters Assn., San Diego Chapter 67

HELMUT SCHMIDT, DR., Institut for Zoologie, University of Bonn 58

LINNEA SPEARS 23, 28, 40

BOB STEELE 59

SUSAN STROM 10

JAN VAN WAGTENDONK, U.S. Geological Survey Yosemite Field Station 54

HAROLD WEAVER, courtesy of Harold Biswell Jr. 33

YOSEMITE NATIONAL PARK MUSEUM, National Park Service, George Reichel 37a, Dan Taylor 37b

Figures

FIGURES 1–3, 5, 6, 8, 10, in the public domain.

FIGURE 4, redrawn from Sugihara et al. 2006.

FIGURE 7, Smokey Bear Fire Prevention Campaign, USDA Forest Service

FIGURE 9, the Boondocks © 2003 Aaron McGruder. Dist. by Universal Press Syndicate. Reprinted with permission. All rights reserved.

Maps

MAPS 1, 4, 7, 8, 12, redrawn from California Department of Forestry and Fire Protection, Fire, and Resource Assessment Program.

MAP 2, courtesy of Jan van Wagtendonk, Research Forester, U.S. Geological Survey Yosemite Field Station.

MAP 3, redrawn from California Department of Fish and Game, 2003.

MAP 5, redrawn from Quinn and Keeley 2006.

MAP 6, redrawn from U.S. Department of Agriculture, Forest Service, 1990.

MAP 9, courtesy of Richard Minnich, Earth Sciences Department, University of California, Riverside.

MAP 10, courtesy of Max Moritz, Environmental Science, Policy, and Management Department, University of California, Berkeley.

MAP 11, redrawn from CAL FIRE Fire Hazard Severity Zone Maps, 2007.

ADDITIONAL CAPTIONS

TITLE PAGE, ii–iii   Low water pressure was a major problem during the Laguna Beach fire in 1993.

PART OPENER, pp. xvi–1   Flames are visual evidence of fire.

PART OPENER, pp. 26–27   After chaparral shrubs burned, California poppies *(Eschscholzia californica)* and blue dicks *(Dichelostemma capitatum)* flowered near Lake Berryessa.

INDEX

ABOUT THE AUTHOR

David Carle received a bachelor's degree from the University of California at Davis in wildlife and fisheries biology and a master's degree from California State University at Sacramento in recreation and parks administration. He was a ranger for the California State Parks for 27 years. He worked at various sites, including the Mendocino Coast, Hearst Castle, the Auburn State Recreation Area, the State Indian Museum in Sacramento, and, from 1982 through 2000, the Mono Lake Tufa State Reserve. He has taught biology and natural history courses at Cerro Coso Community College (the Eastern Sierra College Center) in Mammoth Lakes. David has written several books, among them *Introduction to Air in California* and *Introduction to Water in California* (University of California Press, 2006 and 2004), *Water and the California Dream: Choices for the New Millennium* (Sierra Club Books, 2003), *Burning Questions: America's Fight with Nature's Fire* (Praeger, 2002), and *Mono Lake Viewpoint* (Artemisia Press, 1992).

Series Design:	Barbara Haines
Design Enhancements:	Beth Hansen
Design Development:	Jane Tenenbaum
Cartography:	Lohnes & Wright
Illustration:	Dartmouth Publishing
Composition:	Jane Rundell
Indexing:	Thérèse Shore
Text:	9.5/12 Minion
Display:	ITC Franklin Gothic Book and Demi
Printing and binding:	Golden Cup Printing Company Limited

Introduction to California Mountain Wildflowers, Revised Edition, by Philip A. Munz, edited by Dianne Lake and Phyllis M. Faber

Introduction to California Spring Wildflowers of the Foothills, Valleys, and Coast, Revised Edition, by Philip A. Munz, edited by Dianne Lake and Phyllis M. Faber

Introduction to Shore Wildflowers of California, Oregon, and Washington, Revised Edition, by Philip A. Munz, edited by Dianne Lake and Phyllis Faber

Introduction to California Desert Wildflowers, Revised Edition, by Philip A. Munz, edited by Diane L. Renshaw and Phyllis M. Faber

Introduction to California Plant Life, Revised Edition, by Robert Ornduff, Phyllis M. Faber, and Todd Keeler-Wolf

Introduction to California Chaparral, by Ronald D. Quinn and Sterling C. Keeley, with line drawings by Marianne Wallace

Introduction to the Plant Life of Southern California: Coast to Foothills, by Philip W. Rundel and Robert Gustafson

Introduction to Horned Lizards of North America, by Wade C. Sherbrooke

Introduction to the California Condor, by Noel F. R. Snyder and Helen A. Snyder

Regional Guides

Natural History of the Point Reyes Peninsula, by Jules Evens

Sierra Nevada Natural History, Revised Edition, by Tracy I. Storer, Robert L. Usinger, and David Lukas